BLUEPRINT FOR MATURITY

BLUEPRINT FOR MATURITY

BOB YANDIAN

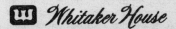 Whitaker House

BLUEPRINT FOR MATURITY

Bob Yandian
Bob Yandian Ministries
P.O. Box 55236
Tulsa, OK 74155–1236

ISBN: 0-88368-355-5
Printed in the United States of America
Copyright © 1985, 1995 by Bob Yandian

Whitaker House
580 Pittsburgh Street
Springdale, PA 15144

Contents

Introduction

The book of Ephesians is one of the most concentrated doctrinal epistles that Paul wrote. Ephesians is one of four such letters written during Paul's first Roman imprisonment: Ephesians, Philippians, Colossians, and Philemon.

During Paul's second missionary journey, he wrote his first epistles, our New Testament books of First and Second Thessalonians. The theme of these two books is the return of the Lord. During his third missionary journey, he wrote the books of Galatians, First and Second Corinthians, and Romans on the theme of spiritual maturity, or growing up in the Lord.

Paul wrote his last letters during his second Roman imprisonment—Titus and the two epistles to Timothy. These are epistles written to pastors; their theme is personal instruction.

Each letter that Paul wrote addressed a problem in a church or in a personal life, except Ephesians. The church at Ephesus was a mature church and growing in faith and love.

(See Ephesians 1:15.) No problem is addressed. Ephesians is a refreshing book that applies to the entire body of Christ.

Because no specific problem is addressed, some doubt whether the letter was specifically for the Ephesian saints. In some of the oldest manuscripts, the words *"at Ephesus"* are not found in the opening salutation (v. 1). It has been surmised that the epistle began at Ephesus and was passed around to the other churches. The theme of Ephesians is the church.

Ephesians and Colossians are the two most parallel books in the New Testament. Many of the same phrases are found in both books, and we will be referring back and forth between the two. The average reader of the two books might wonder what the difference is between them. Well, Ephesians deals with the body itself—the church—and Colossians deals with the Head of the body—Jesus Christ. The two join together like a head and a body.

Ephesians is divided into two sections: chapters 1 through 3 and chapters 4 through 6. The first section deals with **positional truth**, or who we are in Christ; and, the second section deals with **temporal truth**, or the application of positional truth to life.

The righteousness we possess is brought out in the first half of the book, along with eternal life, our election, our hope, and our redemption. The last half tells us how to be good husbands, wives, children, bosses, employees, and witnesses. What good is the righteousness of God if we are too holy to cook dinner? Eternal life still needs to show up at the job on time and accept responsibility around the house. The book of Ephesians is extremely deep in its spiritual truth, yet it is simple in its application.

Philemon was a rich businessman who lived in the city of Colosse. In fact, the church at Colosse met in his home. He owned many slaves, of which one was named Onesimus. (See Colossians 4:9; Philemon 10.) Onesimus stole some money from his master and ran away to Rome where he spent it all. When he ran out of money, he was thrown into prison and ended up with Paul. Paul led him to the Lord and sent him back with the Epistle of Philemon. As you might guess, the book of Philemon teaches about forgiveness. Along with Onesimus went one of Paul's friends, Tychicus (Ephesians 6:21), who delivered the letters of Ephesians and Colossians.

The city of Ephesus was a seaport on the Aegean Sea, one of the great trade and commerce cities of the ancient world. It was a city visited by many travelers and businessmen, and it was built around sexual pleasure. Ephesus was most popular in the ancient world for the worship of Diana, the goddess of fertility.

There was a large temple built in the city dedicated to her worship which drew people from all over the known world at that time. Even though there were other striking facilities in Ephesus, such as large race courses and theaters, the temple of Diana outranked them in popularity. Diana was worshipped through sexual orgies. Pleasure was god to the Greek culture, and sex outside marriage was a perfectly acceptable lifestyle.

That is why much was said about lasciviousness and fornication in the part of the epistle that has been divided into our chapters 4 and 5. Chapter 5 spends a great deal of time on proper marriage relationships. I believe you can begin to see what a difficult place Ephesus would have been to start a church. Along with fornication, idolatry was a way of life. Where idolatry and the works of the flesh function, there are also demons.

Acts 19 tells us the story of Paul's missionary journey into Ephesus. God began the ministry in Ephesus with a great outpouring of the supernatural. Before Paul ever came to the city itself, he met new converts in the upper coasts and led them into the infilling of the Holy Spirit. They spoke with tongues and prophesied when Paul laid hands on them

(Acts 19:6). This begins to tell us of God's approach to the city of Ephesus. The gospel was followed by many signs and wonders.

It was here at Ephesus where *"God wrought special miracles by the hands of Paul: so that from his body were brought unto the sick handkerchiefs or aprons, and the diseases departed from them, and the evil spirits went out of them"* (Acts 19:11–12).

Ephesus is also the place where Satan tried to counterfeit the moving of God through Paul by the seven sons of Sceva. When his plan backfired, *"This was known to all the Jews and Greeks also dwelling at Ephesus; and fear fell on them all, and the name of the Lord Jesus was magnified. And many that believed came, and confessed, and shewed their deeds. Many of them also which used curious arts* [sorcery] *brought their books together, and burned them before all men:...So mightily grew the word of God and prevailed* (Acts 19:17–20). Thus, the book of Ephesians has much to teach us about the Spirit-filled life and our authority over Satan and his kingdom.

Finally, the book of Ephesians is laid out in a systematic and deliberate manner. The main character of chapter 1 is God the Father. The central character of chapter 2 is Jesus Christ. The main character of chapter 3 is the Holy Spirit. The unity and distinction of the

Godhead is seen in the first half of the book where positional truth is the topic.

God the Father is the **originator** of the plan. Jesus Christ is the **executor** of the plan. The Holy Spirit is the **revealer** of the plan. They always have worked this way, no matter what they have done in creation. God the Father designed the plan, and Jesus executed it. God the Father created nothing. Jesus Christ created *"all things...in heaven, and that are in earth, visible and invisible...and he is before* [eternal existence] *all things, and by him all things consist* [are held together]" (Colossians 1:16–17). Jesus Christ created man and angels also, according to the plan of the Father. The Holy Spirit revealed the plan of creation to us through the Word.

Chapters 1 through 3 of Ephesians deal with the plan of redemption and the building of the church. This plan is no different than that of creation. The Father is the originator of the plan of redemption from eternity past. This is the theme of chapter 1. Jesus Christ then went to the cross and executed the plan of redemption, which is the theme of chapter 2. The Holy Spirit is the revealer of the plan of redemption to man. This is the theme of chapter 3.

The plan is given to the church through the fivefold ministry offices, which is the theme of chapter 4. Overcoming sin and putting the Word into use in our everyday lives are explained in chapter 5. Conquest over Satan and our witness to the world are emphasized in chapter 6.

The story of Ephesians is progressive **from** the heart of God **to** the world. How it gets from His heart to us is what we are now about to see.

1

The Plan of God

Ephesians 1:1-14

Verse 1

Paul, an apostle of Jesus Christ by the will of God to the saints which are at Ephesus, and to the faithful in Christ Jesus.

The name Paul means "small" or "little." (See 1 Corinthians 15:9 and Ephesians 3:8.) In looking at ourselves in the natural, we must be like Paul and see ourselves as small. I know that we can *"do all things through Christ"* (Philippians 4:13) and that we are *"more than conquerors"* (Romans 8:37), but this is only through the Greater One living in us and the person of Jesus Himself. We ourselves are small.

Paul, the small one, also calls himself an
apostle. This almost sounds contradictory because of the importance and high standing of
the office of the apostle. *"Paul, an apostle,"*
brings out the two worlds in which we live,
the natural and spiritual. The rest of the verse
also shows this point, *"the saints which are at
Ephesus."* These were natural people who
were called saints. The word *saints* means
"holy ones." Outwardly, you are small and can
fail; but, inwardly, you are a saint and holy.
Paul was outwardly small, but inwardly he was
great. He stood in the office of the apostle.

The Greek word for apostle is *apostolos*,
which means "sent one." This is someone who
is going with a particular mission to a particular destination. Jesus is called *"the Apostle
and High Priest"* (Hebrews 3:1). That means
that He was sent to heaven with a direct mission to take our prayers and words of faith
before the Father. Jesus is sent for the specific
purpose of being our mediator in heaven, of
taking our needs before the Father.

By tracing the word back, we find that it
originated with the Phoenicians. It was a military term from the Phoenician navy. The highest ranking military officer in that branch of
the military was called an "apostle." He would
correspond in rank to our admiral. The word
apostle also means "the one of highest rank."

First Corinthians 12:28 says, *"God hath set some in the church, first apostles, secondarily prophets, thirdly teachers."* The reason Paul numbered them is because he was listing them in their order of importance. The one of highest rank is the apostle.

The Doctrine of Apostleship

Apostleship is a matter of grace and not a talent. Apostleship is not a talent; it is the gift of God. A talent is something with which you are born, such as musical or athletic ability. These things are fine but are not classified in the Word as graces. (See Romans 12:3–4 and Ephesians 4:7.) Grace comes from God the Father. The offices in the body of Christ come from God the Father and from Jesus. Notice again in 1 Corinthians 12:28 it says, *"God hath set some in the church."* Ephesians 4:11 says, *"and he* [Jesus Christ] *gave some..."*

Again, note in the verse that began this chapter, *"Paul, an apostle of Jesus Christ by the will of God."* Galatians 1:1 says, *"Paul, an apostle, (not of men, neither by man, but by Jesus Christ, and God the Father)."* It is not *"by man,"* singular, or *"of men,"* plural. Ministry offices are not appointed by individuals or chosen by committees. It is God the Father and Jesus Christ who set apostles in the church.

At this point, a very controversial issue is usually raised: What about the choosing of Matthias? Was he an apostle or not? Let's look at the first chapter of Acts and see.

Jesus had told His disciples to go and wait in the city of Jerusalem until they were filled with the Holy Spirit. I want you to see something that Jesus did not say: "Go to the upper room, wait for the Holy Spirit, and choose an apostle." Yet that is what they tried to do.

Acts 1:15–26

[15] *And in those days Peter stood up in the midst of the disciples, and said, (the number of names together were about an hundred and twenty,)*

[16] *Men and brethren, this scripture must needs have been fulfilled, which the Holy Ghost by the mouth of David spake before concerning Judas, which was guide to them that took Jesus.*

[17] *For he was numbered with us, and had obtained part of this ministry.*

[18] *Now this man purchased a field with the reward of iniquity, and falling headlong, he burst asunder in the midst, and all his bowels gushed out.*

[19] *And it was known unto all the dwellers at Jerusalem, insomuch as that field is called in their proper tongue, Aceldma*

that is to say, the field of blood.
²⁰ *For it is written in the book of Psalms, Let his habitation be desolate, and let no man dwell therein: and his bishopric let another take.*
²¹ *Wherefore of these men which have companied with us all the time that the Lord Jesus went in and out among us,*
²² *Beginning from the baptism of John, unto that same day that he was taken up from us, must one be ordained to be a witness with us of his resurrection.*
²³ *And they appointed two, Joseph called Barsabas who was surnamed Justus and Matthias.*
²⁴ *And they prayed and said, Thou, Lord, which knowest the hearts of all men, shew whether of these two thou hast chosen,*
²⁵ *That he may take part of this ministry and apostleship, from which Judas by transgression fell, that he might go to his own place.*
²⁶ *And they gave forth their lots; and the lot fell upon Matthias; and he was numbered with the eleven apostles.*

Underline the name Matthias. Draw a circle around it. That is the last time you ever hear of Matthias. He is never mentioned in any other book of the Bible. I think the reason is obvious: he was not chosen by God the Father or the Lord Jesus Christ. He was picked by men and then nominated by the casting of lots.

I believe this is the reason why Paul said in Galatians 1:1, *"not of men* [plural], *neither by man* [singular]." In other words, Paul was saying, "I was not elected by one man, namely Peter. And I was not elected by any group of people, namely the 120. Rather, I was chosen by God the Father and the Lord Jesus Christ." This perfectly lines up with the Scripture that the apostles are chosen by the will of God and by the will of Jesus Christ.

Someone might ask, "Why is the story of Matthias in the Bible anyway?" I believe the story is there to show the fallacy of men and the faithfulness of God. Even though men chose one, God chose another. The Bible is full of people's mistakes from which we can learn. We can understand where they missed it and not make the same mistakes ourselves.

The next question is, "Who replaced Judas?" I believe Paul replaced Judas although there is no definite Scripture that says so. Paul said that he was an apostle chosen by God the Father and the Lord Jesus Christ. In 1 Corinthians 15:7–10, he included himself with the list of apostles who saw the Lord Jesus Christ. He saw him in resurrection on the road to Damascus. He was the one who was chosen *"out of due time"* (v. 8).

Apostles to the Church

We find that apostles to the church were not appointed until after the resurrection of the Lord Jesus Christ:

When He ascended up on high, he... gave gifts unto men...apostles...for the perfecting of the saints.
(Ephesians 4:8, 11, 12)

And when he had called unto him his twelve disciples, he gave them power against unclean spirits, to cast them out, and to heal all manner of sickness and all manner of disease.   (Matthew 10:1)

These twelve Jesus sent forth, and commanded them, saying, Go not into the way of the Gentiles, and into any city of the Samaritans enter ye not: But go rather to the lost sheep of the house of Israel.   (Matthew 10:5–6)

These Scriptures show that the twelve disciples at the time of Jesus' public ministry were not given the same ministry as those chosen after His resurrection. The apostles in Ephesians 4 are given to the church for the perfecting of the saints. The office of apostle today is not the same as the office of apostle under the public ministry of Jesus. If it were, why would Jesus give something which already existed? Only one thing remains constant: Jesus Christ still chooses ministry officers. Men do not.

The office of apostle is found many times in the New Testament epistles. A number of men were called to that office: Barnabas (Acts 14:14), James (Galatians 1:19 and 1 Corinthians 15:7), Apollos (1 Corinthians 4:6–9), and Silvanus and Timothy (1 Thessalonians 1:1 and 2:6) are only a few of the many mentioned in the Scriptures. To be consistent with Scripture, I have to say that these apostles were chosen by God and not by men, but men were used to bear witness that these men had been chosen by God.

Some may be asking, Do we still have apostles today? Well, do we have "sent ones" today? If apostles were given to the church *"for the perfecting of the saints,"* I ask you, Does the church still exist today, and do saints still need to be perfected today? The answer to all of these questions is, "Yes!"

Apostles today fulfill the office of the missionary. Apostles are ministry pioneers in certain regions of the world, setting up churches after they have won the lost to the Lord. I do not consider all missionaries to be apostles, but I do consider all apostles to be missionaries.

So often we look at missionaries who have spent years on foreign fields as "low on the totem pole." However, God considers them to be the "ones of highest rank." We need to quit looking at people through our own eyes and see them through God's.

Along with the office of apostle, as well as all ministry offices, come spiritual gifts. Romans 11:29 says, *"For the gifts and calling of God are without repentance."* Gifts and callings go hand in hand. We often desire to be in a certain ministry office because of the way someone blesses us who stands in that calling. We often desire to operate in spiritual gifts like someone else does because of the blessing they were to us or to someone else that we know. Instead, we need to be on our knees seeking God as to where we fit as individuals in the body of Christ. When we become comfortable in our calling (no matter how small it may seem in the natural), God will give us the spiritual gifts to accompany that office. The gifts and calling are both of God.

First Corinthians 12:4–6 explains this even more clearly. *"Now there are diversities of gifts, but the same spirit"* (v. 4). This tells us that the Holy Spirit manages the gifts. *"And there are differences of administrations* [offices], *but the same Lord"* (v. 5). This tells us that the Lord Jesus governs the ministry offices. *"And there are diversities of operations, but it is the same God which worketh all in all"* (v. 6). It is God the Father who works all the gifts in all the offices. God the Father mixes all the gifts of the Holy Spirit with all the offices of Jesus Christ. *"For the gifts and calling of God are without repentance."*

Find your calling first. God will give the proper gifts of the Spirit to enhance the office in which you stand. In *"covet*[ing] *earnestly the best gifts"* (1 Corinthians 12:31), we should do so to amplify and bring to full fruition the ministry gift inside of us. The apostle will operate in different gifts than the pastor or evangelist. Each should not be jealous of the other because God works *"all in all."*

Let's look once again at the opening salutation of this letter from Paul to the Ephesian church:

> ¹ *Paul, an apostle of Jesus Christ by the will of God, to the saints which are at Ephesus, and to the faithful in Christ Jesus.*

In comparison, the opening greeting of Colossians reads, *"Paul, an apostle of Jesus Christ by the will of God...To the saints and faithful brethren in Christ which are at Colosse"* (vv. 1, 2). (Since Ephesians and Colossians parallel one another, we will be comparing them throughout this book.)

Paul points out that at Ephesus as well as at Colosse, there are saints. Within the ranks of the saints are the faithful. That describes most churches that we have today. Most of the people in the churches are born again; they are saints. But within the numbers of saved church-attendees are the faithful. This is the church within the church, the dedicated core. From these come the faithful workers and eventually the full-time ministers for whom God is looking. Thus, this letter is to all of the saints but especially to the faithful ones.

Verse 2

Grace be unto you, and peace, from God our Father, and from the Lord Jesus Christ.

This is a familiar salutation repeated in much of the New Testament. (See Romans 1:7, 1 Corinthians 1:3, 2 Corinthians 1:2, Galatians 1:3, Philippians 1:2, Colossians 1:2, *et al.*) Notice that grace always comes before peace. Before you can have peace in your life, you have to understand the grace of God.

I have seen people who are so wrapped up in their own self-efforts that they never have peace. They remain frustrated. They are trying to work to please God. However, the thing about working to please God is that you never know when you have done enough or performed well enough to meet His requirements. The devil will tell you, "You could have prayed longer. You could have gone to one more church service. God is not pleased with you." This will always leave you frustrated and without peace.

But when you understand His grace, when you understand that God has already done all the work, then all you need to do is receive His gifts of grace. All the pressure is off, and peace is the result.

Second Peter 1:2 points out that grace and peace can be multiplied to us through knowledge of Jesus Christ. Understanding of God's Word always increases our capacity to handle more of His blessings. As we increase our capacity, God increases the amount He gives.

David said, *"my cup runneth over"* (Psalm 23:5). God always fills to overflowing, but He only pours out when we have something with which to receive. If you do not have a cup, God is under no obligation to pour. The cup comes through knowledge of God and His Word. As your knowledge increases, your cup increases. Increased capacity brings increased blessings.

God's Plan Laid Out

Verses 3–14

³ *Blessed be the God and Father of our Lord Jesus Christ, who hath blessed us with all spiritual blessings in heavenly places in Christ:*

⁴ *According as he hath chosen us in him before the foundation of the world, that we should be holy and without blame before him in love:*

⁵ *Having predestinated us unto the adoption of children by Jesus Christ to himself, according to the good pleasure of his will,*

⁶ *To the praise of the glory of his grace, wherein he hath made us accepted in the beloved.*

⁷ *In whom we have redemption through his blood, the forgiveness of sins, according to the riches of his grace;*

⁸ *Wherein he hath abounded toward us in all wisdom and prudence;*

⁹ *Having made known unto us the mystery of his will, according to his good pleasure which he hath purposed in himself:*

¹⁰ *That in the dispensation of the fulness of times he might gather together in one all things in Christ, both which*

*are in heaven, and which are on earth;
even in him:*
[11] In whom also we have obtained an inheritance, being predestinated according to the purpose of him who worketh all things after the counsel of his own will:
[12] That we should be to the praise of his glory, who first trusted in Christ.
[13] In whom ye also trusted, after that ye heard the word of truth, the gospel of your salvation: in whom also after that ye believed, ye were sealed with that holy Spirit of promise,
[14] Which is the earnest of our inheritance until the redemption of the purchased possession, unto the praise of his glory.

The reason such a long section is taken at this time is because of the sentence structure in the Greek. Verses 3 through 14 are all one sentence in the Greek. Even though there is a period in this section in your *King James Version* after verse 12, there is no pause in the Greek. This is all one sentence, one thought, in the mind of God.

Everything discussed in these verses of Scripture was the plan of God for us before the foundation of the world. Before the earth, universe, or angels were created, God had already formulated the plan of redemption and all of its rewards and gifts.

I want you to imagine a day in time billions and billions of years before the universe existed. No earth or angels existed, only the Godhead itself. They are all eternal and co-equal. God the Father called a conference and told of His plan for creation and redemption of mankind. When the conference was over, God's plan was settled and complete. He needed no one else to help. The plan was as strong and eternal as He Himself is.

I want you to notice that in all of these Scriptures, the action God took is past tense. In verse 3, He *"hath blessed us"*; in verse 4, He *"hath chosen us"*; in verse 5, *"having predestinated us"*; in verse 6, He *"hath made us accepted"*; in verse 7, we *"have redemption"*; in verse 8, He *"hath abounded toward us"*; in verse 9, *"having made known unto us the mystery of his will"*; in verse 11, we *"have obtained an inheritance"*; in verse 13, we *"were sealed with the holy Spirit of promise"*; and, in verse 14, we *"were given the earnest* [down payment] *of our inheritance."*

All these things were done for us before the foundation of the world. The immediate question you might ask is, How could God do all these things for me when I was not even here? The answer is because we had an elected representative, Jesus Christ. God poured all these blessings on the Son, and

they were held in Him until our redemption
day. Notice that each one of these verses is
qualified. In verse 3, He *"hath blessed us...in
Christ"*; in verse 4, He *"hath chosen us in
him"*; in verse 5, *"having predestinated us...by
Jesus Christ"*; in verse 6, He *"hath made us
accepted in the beloved."*

Every blessing we have in time or eternity
is made possible because of the Lord Jesus
Christ. All blessings from God come through
Him, and all our blessings back to the Father
go through Him. He is our mediator, the
God-man. Righteous God and fallen man can
become one through Jesus Christ.

The next obvious question is, Why did He
do all these things for me before I was here?
Why didn't He wait for me to come before
doing all these things? The answer is, So you
could not help! God did these things for you so
you could not assist Him. He did not need
your help, so He formulated the plan of redemption and eternal blessings before the
foundation of the world.

If God had included man in the foundation of the plan, it would have failed. A plan is
only as strong as its weakest link. With God
and man, man would be the weak link. If any
part of God's plan was dependent on man, it
would not be a perfect plan. Man is imperfect
and therefore would weaken the plan of God.

Man accepts a perfect plan which cannot fail. It was planned by God and for God, who is its Author and Finisher.

Have you ever tried to help God? We all have. As I was flying on a commercial jet to a meeting in Michigan once, I had to change planes in Dallas. As we were taxiing onto the runway, the captain pointed out one of the new supersonic Concorde jets about to take off from the runway. He said the plane would fly from Dallas to Paris in 3½ hours at twice the speed of sound. As we were continuing on to Michigan, I thought about that Concorde flying more than twice as fast as we were, and I began to wish we were flying that fast. Then the thought hit me, What can I do about it, get out and push? All I could do was sit back and enjoy the ride. Helping God is like getting out and pushing—useless. Sit back and enjoy the ride because God is in control.

Verse 3

Blessed be the God and Father of our Lord Jesus Christ, who hath blessed us with all spiritual blessings in heavenly places in Christ.

Verse 3 is a praise to God the Father. Notice that we bless Him because He has blessed us. God always takes the initiative, and we respond. Praise acclaims God for what He has done. Worship acclaims Him for who He is, our great heavenly Father.

This verse tells us also that our blessings are spiritual and in heavenly places. There are two reasons for this. First, there was no physical creation at the time God decreed the plan of redemption. This was done before the foundation of the world. The only type of blessings God could have given to us through Christ were spiritual blessings. This was what we needed first, spiritual blessings. We were seen through the halls of time as *"dead in our trespasses and sins"* (Ephesians 2:1). Long before any physical blessings are given to us, God deals with the real root of all of our problems, spiritual death.

Secondly, all physical blessings have their roots in spiritual blessings. The natural world is a mirror image of the spiritual world. God created this earth with all its physical beauty to look like the spiritual world He lives in called heaven. The natural world around us was created by a spiritual force, the words from God's mouth. (See Genesis 1:3–26 and Hebrews 11:3.) So, this verse begins with the source of all our blessings in life and eternity, with spiritual blessings in heavenly places.

Verse 4

According as he hath chosen us in him before the foundation of the world, that we should be holy and without blame before him.

Notice again when we were chosen— *"before the foundation of the world."* This shows us once again the immensity of God, who has always existed. There never was a time nor ever will be a time when He will not exist. Time is no problem with Him because He lives in a realm where time does not exist. We are bound by time, but God is not. He sees tomorrow, next year, and eternity to come as clearly as we see this moment. He knows the problems you will face tomorrow and has already planned every answer for you. God planned answers before problems existed. It is close to blasphemy to think that you are going to face a problem tomorrow or next week for which God has not already made a way of escape (1 Corinthians 10:13).

Problems may catch you off-guard, but they never surprise God. If He planned for the biggest problem in your life through the new birth, don't you think He can handle the smaller ones on the job, in the home, or at school? Somehow we get the idea that God

saved us, filled us with the Holy Spirit, and left
us to fend for ourselves. God not only planned
for us to enter this new life but also to be a
success every day after. Has God ever let you
down? Then will He ever let you down? No!

Worry usually is future-oriented. "God
has taken care of me every single day up to
today, but tomorrow it will all go under." God
knows the future and has made plans for you
to succeed. Don't try to help God by worrying.
Sit back and enjoy the ride. This is the life of
faith that pleases God. (See Hebrews 11:6.)

The verb *"hath chosen"* is from the Greek
word *kalleo* and means "to call out." Before the
foundation of the world, God "called out" your
name as *"holy and without blame."* From the
foundation of the world, He has seen you
through His eyes as righteous and holy. We need
to see ourselves as God sees us.

> *While we look not at the things which
> are seen* [our mistakes and failures],
> *but at the things which are not seen*
> [our heavenly position]: *for the things
> which are seen are temporal; but the
> things which are not seen are eternal.*
>   (2 Corinthians 4:18)

Right now, seated with Jesus in heaven,
you are seen as *"holy and without blame"*

because you are in Him (Christ). You cannot get any more holy spiritually, because you are in Him. If you could become more holy spiritually, then that would mean that Jesus could become more holy; but, Jesus is as holy and without blame as God the Father. And that is the limit of holiness. Therefore, if I am in Him, I am *"holy and without blame."*

What does this concept mean? It means that even if I miss it in life, God still considers me holy and without blame before Him. This in no way advocates my sinning or living an unholy life. What it does is to remove the attitude of defeat if you do sin or miss the mark. Just realize that God hates sin and ask Him to forgive you (1 John 1:9), then see yourself as He does—forgiven, holy, and without blame.

Verse 5

(...in love:) Having predestinated us unto the adoption of children by Jesus Christ to himself, according to the good pleasure of his will.

Notice that this verse should begin with *"in love."* In the *King James* translation, this phrase appears at the end of verse 4. *"In love"* really amplifies the meaning of predestination, not our righteous standing.

Predestination is a highly misunderstood subject. The concept has run the gamut of reactions from ridicule to praise from one source to another. The Greek word for predestination is *proorizo* and means to "predesign." Predestination does not mean "foreordination." In other words, it does not mean that God has your life planned ahead for you and that you have no say about it. Your will is precious to God because you were made in His image and He has will. In fact, **your will is the foundation for predestination.** Predestination is not the foundation, God's foreknowledge is the foundation. *"For whom he did foreknow, he also did predestinate"* (Romans 8:29). Only believers are predestinated, never unbelievers.

God looked down the corridor of time and saw you. He first found you dead in your sins and planned for His Son Jesus to go to the cross and die for your redemption. Then He saw you presented with the choice of eternal life at some point and knew whether you would accept Jesus Christ or not. If you rejected the Son, there was no plan for your life, only an eternity under the penalty of the wrath of God (John 3:36). If you did receive Jesus Christ as your Lord and Savior, you entered into His plan of predestination. Redemption is potential. It is your decision that makes it a reality. *"Who gave himself for our sins, that he might deliver us from this present evil world"* (Galatians 1:4).

After our salvation, our will is just as important to the Father as it was before we were born again. Our will caused us to enter into His plan and is the secret for victory every day thereafter. *"Whereby are given unto us exceeding great and precious promises: that by these* [promises] *ye might be partakers of the divine nature"* (2 Peter 1:4). After we have received the divine nature, we need to partake of it. This is done through faith in His exceeding great and precious promises. Again, this is only potential for us. It is up to us to believe His Word.

Verse 5 is telling us that God had a plan for us to be His children. The new birth was part of His eternal plan so that He could have a whole family as precious to Him as His firstborn Son, Jesus Christ. *"For whom he did foreknow, he also did predestinate to be conformed to the image of his Son, that he might be the firstborn among many brethren"* (Romans 8:29).

I especially enjoy reading the end of the fifth verse because it tells us why God predestinated us—*"according to the good pleasure of his will."* He did it because He wanted to. No one was there to coerce Him or twist His arm. What a great heavenly Father we have, who loved us so much!

Verse 6

*To the praise of the glory of his grace,
wherein he hath made us accepted in
the beloved.*

The motivation of God is always grace,
which is the nature of God Himself. Grace is
always dependent on who and what God is,
never on who or what man is. God blesses us
on His merits, not ours. This causes all the
praise and adoration to go to Him who created
and gives the blessings, never to man who
simply receives them. The reason we praise
God the Father is because He has made us accepted in His Son Jesus Christ (the Beloved).
There is no other place of acceptance with
God except in His Son. The Son is the only
place of favor God has ordained in heaven and
earth.

In ourselves, we can never be accepted
with God, no matter how many works and
deeds we do in this earth. *"But we are all as
an unclean thing, and all our righteousnesses*
[good works] *are as filthy rags"* (Isaiah 64:6).
God was pleased with His Son Jesus from the
foundation of the world and has always been
pleased with everything He has ever done or
will ever do. Throughout His entire lifetime,
Jesus always sought to please His Father. In

death, burial, resurrection, and ascension, God the Father was satisfied and appeased with the work of His Son. Consequently, there is only one place of acceptance with God, and that is in the Son. At the point of our faith in Christ, God places us in union with Him, and we share in the acceptance of Christ. We are then *"accepted in the Beloved."*

Verse 7

In whom [the Beloved, Jesus Christ] *we have redemption through his blood, the forgiveness of sins, according to the riches of His grace.*

Again, it is only *"in Him"* that we have any blessings at all, including redemption and forgiveness.

The word *redemption* means "to buy back." We were owned by the Lord at one time and, through sin, we were lost to Him after Adam's transgression. Jesus came into this world as the *"last Adam"* (1 Corinthians 15:45) to go to the cross and pay the ransom price through the shedding of His blood on the cross. The wages of sin is death, and man did not have the price to pay in order to free himself. Jesus' blood represented His life because *"the life of the flesh is in the blood...for it is the blood that maketh an atonement for the soul"* (Leviticus 17:11). He gave His life, which was perfect and without blemish, for us so that we who were with blemish and spot could have redemption and forgiveness of sins.

When Adam sinned, he lost his position with God and threw the rest of mankind into slavery. Adam and Eve were slaves to Satan and the flesh because of the sin nature that entered into them through their disobedience and the resulting fall from Eden and being under the curse. Slaves can only give birth to slaves. Every man and woman born into this earth through natural parents is a slave. Slaves beget slaves. Slaves cannot free slaves because freedom has to be purchased. Slaves receive no wages and therefore have no ransom price to free themselves, let alone every other slave. It takes a free man to set free slaves.

Adam and Eve began as free but voluntarily walked into the slave market. Mohammed cannot free mankind because he was a slave. Sun Myung Moon, Confucius, Joseph Smith, Mary Baker Eddy, or anyone you can name cannot free themselves, let alone a group or denomination, because they were, or are, all slaves. The only free man since Adam and Eve on this earth has been Jesus Christ. Through the virgin birth, He came into this earth free from the nature of the flesh and the penalty of sin. He was the only man qualified to redeem mankind. On the cross, He redeemed us; He bought us back. We are twice His—the first, lost in Adam, and the second, redeemed in Jesus.

Once He redeemed us, He forgave us of our original sin in Adam and all acts of sin we have ever committed. He forgives us *"according to the riches of His grace."* How infinite is His grace? It cannot be calculated. The riches of His grace cannot be exhausted even if all men on the earth were to partake at one time. That is the standard He uses to forgive us. No sin you have ever committed or will commit exists that He cannot or will not forgive.

If there is a sin that cannot be forgiven, then sin is greater than grace. That thought is blasphemous. If you had at your disposal an infinite checking account, there could never be a bill or debt large enough to cause you to go bankrupt. Don't let the devil browbeat you and tell you that your sins have been so bad that God no longer loves you or will not forgive you. You remind Satan that your sins are forgiven *"according to the riches of His grace."* For Satan to bankrupt heaven, he would have to be bigger than God. God's mercy, which is grace in action, endures forever.

Verse 8

Wherein [in grace] *he hath abounded toward us in all wisdom and prudence.*

This verse is probably the best definition of grace I have ever found. I have heard and used all the standard definitions such as "unmerited favor" and "God's riches at Christ's expense," but this verse really revealed to me God's definition of grace. **Grace at its simplest is God abounding toward man.** God does everything. Man simply receives. Imagine yourself standing still while God runs or abounds toward you with everything that pertains to life and godliness. Everything you need for your natural and spiritual existence in this life and throughout eternity is being delivered to you by God the Father.

Not only does He give us natural and spiritual blessings, but He also gives the ability to flow supernaturally in our everyday situations. He gives us wisdom and prudence (good sense). Both of these attributes are products of the Spirit-filled and Word-filled life.

Wisdom is the correct application of knowledge. Knowledge is an input, and wisdom is an output. Knowledge is being a hearer of the Word, and wisdom is being a doer. Knowledge is gained through our being diligent. We must study to show ourselves approved unto God (2 Timothy 2:15). God will not do this for us. Once we have done our part and studied, God will help us put what we have learned to work in the form of wisdom. The Word does not say, *"If any man lack knowledge, let him ask of God."* It does say, *"If any man lack wisdom, let him ask of God"* (James 1:5).

Not only does God give us wisdom, but He also gives us good sense or prudence. Christians should make more sense than anyone in the world. Believers full of the Word should come up with such common-sense decisions that the world would stand in awe as to why they could not see the simplicity of the answer.

Verse 8 should be a daily confession of every believer: "My God is abounding toward me today with wisdom and good sense for every circumstance and problem that I will face today." There is not a weapon formed against you that can prosper when you are armed with the simplicity of the Word of God (Isaiah 54:17).

Verse 9

Having made known unto us the mystery of his will, according to his good pleasure which he hath purposed in himself.

Here, the Greek says, *"having* [already] *made known."* The action described in verse 9 took place before the action of verse 8. In other words, He made known unto us the mystery of His will, and then He abounded toward us with wisdom and good sense.

God would not come to us with a gift until He first let us know that He was coming and what He had to give to us. God is a perfect gentleman. He gives us plenty of information about what He has for us so we can anticipate and have our faith built up to receive. The preaching of the gospel prepares the hearts of men to receive the gift of eternal life. God does all of this *"according to His good pleasure."* He does these things because He wants to, not because someone twists His arm or pressures Him. God does nothing through coercion but according to His own desire.

What God gave us is called in this verse, *"the mystery of His will."* The mystery is discussed further in chapter 3 when Paul goes more into depth about his calling and the message to the Gentiles. For right now, a broad meaning of the word "mystery" will clear up its use in this verse.

"Mystery" means something which was hidden in the past but now is revealed. Many of the blessings we have in the church age were unknown in the Old Testament. God knew of

the church and its time of manifestation, and reserved many gifts for members of the body of Christ which Old Testament saints, prophets, and ministers did not know about. He has made known unto us *"the mystery of His will."*

Verse 10

That in the dispensation of the fullness of times he might gather together in one all things in Christ, both which are in heaven, and which are on earth; even in him:

"The dispensation (singular) *of the fullness of times* (plural)*"* is the millennium. God's purpose is that in the millennial reign of the Lord Jesus Christ to come, He might gather together everything in heaven and everything on earth into one kingdom. He will do all this through His Son.

Right now, heaven is in divine order under the reign of God Himself. On earth we have a different story. There are two kingdoms on the earth headed by two leaders, Jesus Christ and Satan. Jesus is the Head of the church, and Satan is the god of this world. Believers in the Lord Jesus are in the world but not of it. (See John 17:11–16.) There is going to come a day when Satan's kingdom will be destroyed by the coming of Jesus to take His rightful throne. Jesus will rule and reign on the earth as He has ruled in heaven. Heaven and earth will function as one kingdom, and we will be ruling and reigning with the Lord Jesus Himself. This has been the end result of God's plan throughout all the ages of the Old Testament and New.

Verse 11

In whom [Christ] *also we have obtained an inheritance, being predestinated according to the purpose of him who worketh all things after the counsel of his own will.*

An inheritance is the possession of an heir. Being an heir is not something that anyone can work for but something which is the rightful possession of birth. Inheritance is based on family ties, not on self-effort. *"And if children, then heirs"* (Romans 8:17). When we were placed in union with Christ, we became heirs of God and joint heirs with His Son. This verse also tells us that our inheritance was planned by God as a part of the package of predestination. God planned the inheritance before the children were ever born. We might do well to learn from God's example. God is a God of faith, yet He still plans for the future.

Faith is not forgetting the future, making no plans, and expecting everything magically to fall into place. If our example of faith is God Himself, then let us wisely consider His ways.

Verses 12–13

> [12] *That we should be to the praise of his glory, who first trusted* [hoped] *in Christ.* [13] *In whom ye also trusted* [hoped], *after that ye heard the word of truth, the gospel of your salvation: in whom also after that ye believed, ye were sealed with that holy Spirit of promise.*

The translators of the *King James Version* in this passage really missed the point as far as I am concerned. The word *"trusted"* here is the Greek word *proelpizo* and should have been translated "hoped." (You will probably find it in your Bible margin.)

Hope is a misunderstood word today. Most people think of hope as wishful thinking. Many times I have prayed for someone who is sick and asked them after the prayer, "Are you healed?" They will reply, "I hope so." That is not hope; that is a wish. They might as well say, "I wish it were true, but I doubt it." Hope is steadfast confidence. Hope comes from the same place that faith does—the

Word of God. Notice our verse says that we
first hope *"after that ye heard the word of
truth, the gospel of your salvation."* Faith
comes by hearing the Word (Romans 10:17),
but so does *hope.* In fact, this verse tells us
that after we hear the Word of truth, hope
comes before faith: *"in whom also after that ye
believed* [had faith]."

Hope is like a dream, a vision, or a goal. It
is the target for which our faith shoots. Without hope, faith has nothing to look at. Hope is
like an architect's drawings for a new building. The drawing is not the building, but it
gives the workers something to look at and
build from. The drawing represented the
dream. Hope is the dream, and faith makes
the dream come true. You cannot have one
without the other.

*"What things soever ye desire, when ye
pray, believe that ye receive them, and ye shall
have them"* (Mark 11:24). Your desire is your
hope; believing is your faith. Without a desire,
believing is in vain.

Hope is a goal setter. The thermostat on
the wall is like hope in that it, too, is a goal
setter. The thermostat cannot attain the
proper temperature. It can only set the desire
so the heating unit can attain the proper
atmosphere. The thermostat is powerless; so
is hope. The heating unit has the power; so

does faith. Faith has the power to attain the goal set by hope. Faith gives substance to the things hoped for (Hebrews 11:1).

Hope is of the soul, and faith is of the spirit. *"But let us, who are of the day, be sober, putting on the breastplate of faith and love; and for an helmet, the hope of salvation"* (1 Thessalonians 5:8). Faith is called here a breastplate. The breastplate covers the chest, or the spirit. Hope is compared to the helmet. The helmet covers the head, the mind or the soul. *"Which hope we have as an anchor of the soul"* (Hebrews 6:19).

Our mind or soul is useful and important to set goals in life. Our goals should come from the Word just as does our faith. But our mind is powerless to attain these goals. This is where we need to depend on the power from our inward man to bring these hopes, visions, desires, and dreams to pass. Hope comes from the Word and gives faith something to shoot for. If you give up hope during the fight, your faith has nothing to shoot for. *"Hope deferred* [put off] *maketh the heart sick* [weak]*"* (Proverbs 13:12).

"Ye were sealed with that holy Spirit of promise." A seal in the ancient world was engraved into the ring of someone in authority such as a king. When the king sent a personal letter to someone, he put a drop of candle

wax on the flap of the folded letter and sealed it with his crest by pressing his ring into the warm wax. This seal meant two things: this was the king's private property, and only authorized recipients could open the letter.

We are sealed with the Holy Spirit, God's own personal stamp of approval. This means we are the personal property of the King of Kings, and anyone else (namely Satan) ought to keep his hands off. He will invoke the personal wrath of the King if he tampers with His property. We are sealed until Jesus comes back for us at the rapture of the church.

Verse 14

Which [the Holy Spirit] *is the earnest* [down payment] *of our inheritance until the redemption of the purchased possession, unto the praise of his glory.*

The Holy Spirit is the earnest of our inheritance. An earnest is a down payment. When a person buys a piece of property, he may put earnest money down as a guarantee that the remainder of the money is coming. When we were born again, God gave us a down payment on our inheritance in heaven which is yet to come. The down payment is the guarantee that God will come through on the rest of our inheritance. The down payment of our inheritance is the Holy Spirit. Just think, if the down payment is this good, what must the rest of the inheritance be like?

Earnest money is usually just a small portion of the entire purchase price. The Holy Spirit brings us new life, His infilling, comfort in life, communication with the Father, and a supernatural love to those around us. All this is just the down payment on a life to come in heaven which will be even better.

All this will come to pass at the rapture of the church when we rise to meet Jesus in the air. Then we will receive our resurrection bodies, and the final phase of our redemption will be complete. We will receive the full inheritance of the purchased possession. As this verse tells us, it will all be *"unto the praise of his glory."*

The Lord planned our redemption, sent Jesus to the cross to execute the plan, and gave us the Holy Spirit to reveal His will and be the down payment on our inheritance laid up for us in eternity.

2

Paul's Prayer for the Saints

Ephesians 1:15–23

Having written the preceding section of this epistle describing what God did for us before the foundation of the world, Paul then expressed a prayer for the saints at Ephesus. Although this prayer is for a certain group of people in a specific time period, there is no difference between saints then and saints now. We are just as much saints today as they were when Paul wrote this epistle. There is no such thing as the early church and the late church. We are all part of one universal church, the body of the Lord Jesus Christ.

Verses 15–16

[15] *Wherefore I also, after I heard of your faith in the Lord Jesus, and love unto all the saints,*
[16] *Cease not to give thanks for you, making mention of you in my prayers.*

I think it is interesting to note that Paul did not really begin to pray until he heard of their faith and love. That is usually the time when we stop praying. We pray for someone to operate in faith or love and, when they do, we stop praying for them and go to someone else. We need to follow Paul's example in our own lives and put greater effort in our prayers when people come into God's will for their lives. This is the time to pray as Jesus did for Peter, that Satan will not sift their lives as wheat. (See Luke 22:31–32.) Most of the attacks in our lives come because we are doing something right, not because we are doing something wrong. Remember that Paul prayed for the saints at Ephesus after he heard of their *"faith in the Lord Jesus and love unto all the saints."*

Paul also said in this verse that he not only prayed for them but that he also did not cease to give thanks for them. Thanksgiving should be part of our everyday lives as priests before God. (See Ephesians 5:20; Philippians 4:4; and 1 Thessalonians 5:18.) Thanksgiving should be made to the Father for all His goodness to us, and for our brothers and sisters in the body of Christ, especially those who have authority over us. (See Psalm 103:1–2 and 1 Timothy 2:1–4.)

Verse 17

That the God of our Lord Jesus Christ, the Father of glory, may give unto you the [a] *spirit of wisdom and revelation, in the knowledge of him.*

In the Greek, Paul is saying that his desire is for God to give us "[a] *spirit of wisdom and revelation."* Also notice that here the word *"spirit"* begins with a lowercase *s* instead of a capital letter. This tells us that the spirit being spoken of here is not the Holy Spirit. God wants our spirits to be full of wisdom and revelation in the knowledge of Him. Wisdom and revelation are a product of knowledge of God's Word. We are never told in the Scriptures to ask God for knowledge, but we are told to ask Him for wisdom and revelation.

Isaiah 33:6 says, *"And wisdom and knowledge shall be the stability of thy times,*

and strength of salvation." This puts wisdom
and knowledge together. Many people think
knowledge and wisdom are two words which
mean the same thing, but, as we saw before,
they are not. Knowledge is an input, and wisdom is an output. We take in knowledge, but
we produce wisdom.

Wisdom is the correct application of
knowledge. *"If any man lack wisdom let him
ask of God"* (James 1:5). Taking in knowledge
is a discipline for us (2 Timothy 2:15). Once
we do our part, God will bring illumination,
revelation, and wisdom when we ask Him.

Verse 18

> *The eyes of your understanding* [heart]
> *being enlightened; that ye may know
> what is the hope of his calling, and
> what the riches of the glory of his in-
> heritance in the saints.*

Verse 18 now opens the subject that will
be dealt with throughout the remainder of
this chapter. Paul introduces three things he
wants the saints at Ephesus and the saints
today to know. Those three things are named
in verses 18 and 19 and explained in verses
20–23. They are the hope of our calling, the
riches of our inheritance, and the power of

God that raised Jesus from the dead. The first two are found in verse 18. The first is in the future tense and the second, in the present. The third is found in verse 19, and it is in the past tense.

"The eyes of your understanding" is misleading as it appears in the *King James* translation. *"The eyes of your* [heart]" is what the Greek really says. This is a reference to your soul or mind. True illumination or revelation takes place in the mind, not the spirit. Notice that verse 17 told us that we are to have a spirit full of wisdom and revelation. But here in verse 18, we are told that the eyes of our hearts have to be illuminated. Revelation occurs when the wisdom of God, which is resident in our spirit, explodes across our conscious mind. Illumination occurs when the mind and spirit come into unity. You knew it all the time in your spirit, and it finally dawned on your mind. Usually, when this occurs, you say, "I see it!" You do not mean you see it with your natural eyes, but you "see" it with the "eyes of your heart."

As the eyes of our hearts are illuminated, the first thing we perceive is *"the hope of our calling."* We have run across the word *calling* before in verse 4. We were *"chosen* [called out]" in Jesus Christ before the foundation of the world that we should be *"holy and without blame before Him."* Our present verse is telling us that there is coming a day called *"the hope of our calling."* Romans 8 says that this is the day of the redemption of our body or the rapture of the church. On that day, we will be in heaven, physically, just as we are spiritually, *"holy and without blame before Him."*

Right now, we are members of two different worlds, the natural and the spiritual. Spiritually, we are before the Father, holy and without blame, but naturally we are on the earth and still in Satan's world. There is going to come a day when this vile body will be fashioned into the same body as that of the Lord Jesus. We will have resurrection bodies which will have no earthly limits. This mortal body will put on immortality, this corruptible flesh will put on incorruption (1 Corinthians 15:53), and we will stand in heaven before the Father, totally redeemed—spirit, soul, and body. Again, this is called a hope because it is still in the future. The rapture is called the blessed "hope" of the church. (See 1 Thessalonians 4:13–17 and Titus 2:13.) When the world has nothing to look for in the days to come, we can look up and lift our heads up high because our redemption draws nigh (Luke 21:28).

Verse 18 not only tells us what we have coming in the future but also what we have

today, right now, in the devil's world. Many
people talk about how wonderful heaven will
be and how great things used to be. God
knows no time; therefore, today is just as important to Him as yesterday and tomorrow.
God's promises are real every day of our lives.
They are always dependable and will come to
pass for us just as they did for Moses, David,
and Abraham in the past. They will come to
pass for Jesus and all believers in the future
kingdom.

*"And what the riches of the glory of his
inheritance in the saints."* Today, our needs in
this present life are supplied *"according to his
riches in glory by Christ Jesus"* (Philippians
4:19). We have pointed out already that His
riches are inexhaustible and that we can
never have such a great need that it could
bankrupt His account set up for us (Ephesians
1:7). Often though, we think of His riches in
glory as meaning His riches in heaven. When
God supplies a need for us in this lifetime, He
usually does it through a human channel.
This verse confirms this because it tells us
that *"the riches of the glory of his inheritance"*
is *"in the saints."*

He told us that when we give into His
kingdom, He gives it back to us through men
(Luke 6:38). We are taken care of for the future because our hope is the soon return of

the Lord Jesus Christ to take us to heaven to
live with Him. We now know from the last
half of verse 18 that God has taken thought to
supply for us in this lifetime because He has
invested His riches *"in the saints"* to supply
the needs of the body of Christ to fulfill its
mission on the earth. All of this is made possible because of what God did for us through
the death, burial, resurrection, and ascension
of His Son, Jesus. All of our present and future blessings are based on the past work of
the cross.

A Look at Power

Verses 19–20

> [19] *And what is the exceeding greatness of
> his power to us-ward who believe, accord-
> ing to the working of his mighty power,*
> [20] *Which he wrought in Christ, when he
> raised him from the dead, and set him at
> his own right hand in the heavenly places.*

I want to give you five Greek words
translated *"power"* in the New Testament. I
also want to show you the differences among
these words. The first one is the Greek word
dunamis. This is the word from which we get
the English words *dynamo* and *dynamite*. It

means "inherent power" or, literally, "power stored up within something." The second word is *energeia*, which means "outward" or "overt power." We get the English word *energy* from this Greek word.

The difference between those two words is this: If a strong man with big muscles walks into the room, someone might look at him and say, "He sure has power." The word they used would have been *dunamis*; but if he rammed his fist through the wall, they would say, "Sure enough, he has power." This time, they would have use the Greek word *energeia*, because he had displayed his power outwardly. *Energeia* is the display of *dunamis*.

Let's go on to the third word, *kratos*, or "ruling power." Our English word *democratic*, which means "the rule of the people," comes from this word. The fourth word is *ischus*. This word means "endowed power." When a king takes the throne, a certain amount of endowed power is given to him simply because of his office. The fifth word is *exeusia*. Although this word is translated *"power,"* it never should be. It should be translated "authority."

Again, let me point out to you the first four words: *dunamis, energeia, kratos, and ischus*. Every one of these four words is found in verse 19. Needless to say, it is the **most powerful verse** in the entire New Testament.

Also, it is the most difficult verse to translate in all of the New Testament. I have never found any two translations which read the same on this verse. Let me give you this verse, showing the Greek words and their locations:

> [19] *And what is the exceeding greatness of his power* [dunamis] *to us-ward who believe, according to the working* [energeia] *of his mighty* [kratos] *power* [ischus].

What does this verse mean? There was a day in the universe when all of God's **ruling** power, all of God's **endowed** power, and all of God's **inherent** power were put into the form of **energy**. That was the day Jesus Christ was raised from the dead. More power was displayed that one day than had ever been displayed before.

God's Word tells us in various places of the times when God used His power. The main references are to the creation of the universe around us. Psalm 8:3 tells us that when God created the universe and stars, He used His fingers. That's all the effort that it took. We are told in Hebrews 1:10 that when God created the earth, He did it with His hands: *"The foundation of the earth and the heavens* [atmosphere around the earth] *are the works of thine hands."*

Do you have more strength in your hands or in your fingers? In your hands! Have you ever tried to do pushups on your fingertips? You discover very quickly that your hands are more powerful than your fingers. These two verses show us that God used more power to create the earth than He did the universe. We are told in the first chapter of Genesis that God created the heavens and the earth. We are told little about the heavens, but we can learn much about the making of the earth during the six days. God took more time with the earth than He did with the heavens because this was to be the home of His special creatures, man and woman.

Man and woman were created to subdue and take dominion over the earth. The earth and heaven are to work in conjunction with each other. God made man in His image and created a place from which man could rule and reign, which was just like the one where God lived. Earth and heaven look alike. There has not been another planet yet discovered with trees, rivers, or mountains like earth. Heaven also has these things because God made earth in the image of the place where He lives. Whatever we bind on earth is bound in heaven. Whatever we loose on earth is loosed in heaven (Matthew 18:18). God and man are to work together.

Isaiah 53:1 says, *"Who hath believed our report, and to whom is the arm of the Lord revealed?"* Isaiah 53 is the redemption chapter telling of the work of Jesus on the cross to redeem us from sin and sickness. We have moved from the fingers of God to His hands and now to His arm. The arm of the Lord brought us salvation. It took more power for God to redeem us from our sins than it did to create the whole universe and the earth. God needed more power to bring redemption to us because He had no opposition when He created the earth and universe. When He redeemed us, all hell came against Him. *"Having spoiled principalities and powers, he made a show of them openly, triumphing over them in it"* (Colossians 2:15).

For whom did Jesus do all this? It certainly was not for Himself. He had no sin of His own, so He had no need of redemption. He did all of this for us. *"What is the exceeding greatness of his power to us-ward who believe."* That is what Isaiah says in his redemption chapter. The arm of the Lord (*"the exceeding greatness of His power"*) is revealed to those who believe the report (*"us-ward who believe"*). God made the universe and the earth for His own benefit. No one watched Him do it. He redeemed us from Satan for our benefit. When we believe the gospel, we receive the benefits of the exceeding greatness of God's power that raised Jesus from the dead.

Romans 8:11 tells us that the same Spirit which raised Jesus from the dead lives in us and quickens our mortal bodies. Since there was enough power to raise Jesus from the dead, surely there is enough power in us to get rid of cancer, ulcers, or any other form of sickness Satan might throw our way. We have received into our inner being the *"exceeding greatness of God's power."* This power not only raised Jesus from the dead but also set Him at the right hand of God in heaven.

Verse 21

Far above all principality, and power [authority], and might, and dominion, and every name that is named, not only in this world [age], but also in that which is to come.

In verse 21, we have the fifth Greek word that has been translated *"power"—exeusia.* This should have been translated "authority." Through the work of the Lord Jesus Christ on the cross and His resurrection, we have been given authority over the devil.

An obvious question which arises at this point is, What is the difference between power and authority? God has not invested us with power but with authority. In the fall, God did not lose any of His power. What God lost was His channel in the earth for the expression of His power. Adam lost his authority in the earth when he yielded to Satan. From Adam until the cross, Satan had authority on earth.

When Jesus rose from the dead, He said, *"All power [exeusia, authority] is given unto me in heaven and in earth"* (Matthew 28:18). Jesus gave His authority to the church. You are probably thinking that you would rather have power than authority, but that should not be the case. Jesus said in Luke 10:19, *"Behold, I give unto you power [authority] to tread on serpents and scorpions, and over all the power [dunamis] of the enemy: and nothing shall by any means hurt you."* Jesus said he gave us authority over Satan's power.

When a policeman stands on the corner and raises his hand, cars stop because of his authority, not his power. The policeman is not more powerful than the cars and trucks. What would he do if they would not stop? The policeman has been given authority over all the power of the cars. The drivers of the cars will not resist his authority because they know that if they did, they would have to face the power which the policeman represents. The power of the local government is channeled through the authority of the policeman. The policeman does not stand on the corner in his own name but in the name of the law.

Jesus gave us authority over all the power of the enemy. When we use His name, all hell comes to a halt, not because we are so innately powerful, but because we are invested with the authority of heaven. Satan stops for our authority because he does not want to face the power again. He faced the power one day and lost. God channels all the power of heaven through the authority of the believer who knows the rights and privileges that belong to him and are found in the name of Jesus.

The name of Jesus is higher than any other name that can be mentioned in this age (the church age) and also that which is to come (the millennium). The name of Jesus outranks the name of any sickness, disease, problem, world leader, or crisis. We as believers have the right to use that name to cast out devils, speak with new tongues, take up serpents, drink any deadly thing and not be hurt, and lay hands on the sick and see them recover. (See Mark 16:17–18.)

Verse 22

And hath put all things under his feet, and gave him to be the head over all things to the church.

Notice that in verses 21 and 22 Jesus has been put *"far above"* the kingdom of Satan and made to be *"the head over...the church."* If Jesus is far above Satan's kingdom and Satan is below His feet, then something has to be in between. That something between Jesus and Satan is the church. Jesus is not said to be the head of the devil; instead, He is the Head of the church. Then, who is the head of the devil? We are. Jesus has given us authority over Satan. The most unscriptural prayer you can pray is, "Jesus, get rid of the devil for me." He won't do it.

Jesus conquered Satan through the work of the cross and resurrection, and then He gave us the rightful authority to use His name and see the devil run from us. Thank God for the name of Jesus! Satan hates that name, and all of heaven loves to hear it repeated. Every time the name of Jesus is used, both hell and heaven remember that day. Hell trembles and heaven rejoices. We have been left here in the earth to stand in the place that Jesus did (2 Corinthians 5:20) and to see people come to know Jesus as Lord and Savior, Healer, and Provider. Learn to use your authority and to see yourself set free, along with the lives of your friends and loved ones. Jesus has become the Head over all things!

Verse 23

Which [the church] *is his body, the fullness of him that filleth all* [by being] *in all.*

The body of Christ makes up His fullness, just like your body makes up your fullness with your head. Jesus is the Head. We are the body, and together we make up the fullness. He is full with us. We are full with Him. Without Him, we are incomplete, and without us, His kingdom and body would be incomplete. The body of Christ is the fullness of Him (Christ) who fills all (the body of Christ) by being in all (each individual member of the body).

3

How God Found Us

Ephesians 2:1-10

In the first chapter of Ephesians, we learned about the plan of God the Father to redeem us from our sins. Remember that God the Father is the author of the plan, Jesus Christ is the executor of the plan, and the Holy Spirit is the revealer of the plan.

The theme of the second chapter is the work of Jesus on the cross to put the plan of God into effect. Remember that this plan was ordained from the foundation of the world so that God could bring us to Himself as His children. Jesus was the one chosen by God to execute the plan of God. To redeem man from his sins, Jesus would have to suffer the penalty of sin, which is death (Romans 6:23).

Since God saw us as redeemed, chosen, holy, and without blame, He must have seen us with a tremendous need to have designed such a redemption package. Chapter 2 describes how God found us. We were not a pretty sight to look upon because we were lost and dead in our sins. God saw us in a desperate situation before He planned our answers through the blood of Jesus.

In chapter 2, man is seen under a triple curse (vv. 1–3). First, he is under the curse of sin and its penalty. Next, he is under the world's system, ruled by Satan and his forces. Finally, he is under the domination of the unrenewed mind, the nature of the flesh.

Verse 1

And you hath he quickened [made alive]
who were dead in trespasses and sins.

This verse says we *"were dead in trespasses and sins."* *"Trespasses"* in the Greek is the word *paraptoma.* W. E. Vine translates this as "blunder."[1] In other words, this would be "unknown sin." The Greek word for *"sins"* is *hamartia,* which means "known sin." The sinner today is

---

not only lost in the sins he knows about but also in those he does not know to be sin. God made us alive from both types of sins and raised us up through the work of the cross.

Verse 2

Wherein [in sins] *in time past* [before salvation] *ye walked according to the course of this* world [the world's system], *according to the prince of the power of the air, the spirit that now worketh in the children* [the sons] *of disobedience.*

This verse says that when you were a sinner, you walked according to an organized path in this world. Sinners today (as well as many Christians) think they are doing their own thing. Nothing could be further from the truth. They are being manipulated and led by the god of this world, Satan. They are not doing their own thing; they are doing the devil's thing. Satan here is called *"the prince of the power of the air."* He is the prince of the demons, who are the power of the air. The Greek word for *"air"* is *aer* and it means "the atmosphere around the earth."

Sinners are citizens of Satan's world and under the control of his kingdom in this earth.

God has given us as believers the authority to
break the power of Satan and his demons and
to set unbelievers free to become citizens of
heaven. Philippians 3:20 says, *"our conversation* [citizenship] *is in heaven."* We are in the
world but not of it. There was a time when we
changed citizenships and became new crea-
tions in Christ. As citizens of heaven, we have
angels and the power of prayer at our disposal.
Whatever we bind on earth is bound in heaven,
and whatever we loose on earth is loosed in
heaven (Matthew 16:19). We have authority
over *"the prince of the power of the air."*

Do you remember in Daniel, chapter 10,
when the angel was sent in response to Daniel's prayer? How long did it take the angel to
get from heaven to the atmosphere of the
earth? This was done in an instant. But then
it took the angel 21 days to get through the
atmosphere to Daniel. Daniel had prayed for
three weeks, and the angel said he came in
answer to Daniel's prayer (Daniel 10:12).
Through prayer, Daniel had the authority to
hold back the demon forces and to allow the
angel of God to bring the answer to him.

Demons inhabit our atmosphere and earth
as does their leader, Satan. Angels can infil-
trate their domain and bring help from God.
But only men who know God have authority in
the earth.

Verse 3

Among whom [the sons of disobedience] *also we all had our conversation* [manner of life] *in times past in the lusts of our flesh, fulfilling the desires of the flesh and of the mind, and were by nature the children of wrath, even as others.*

This verse says that, before you were born again, you were controlled by the flesh and the mind. Notice that the spirit is left out. Unless the sinner is demon-possessed, he is not controlled by his spirit. He is under the control of the nature of the flesh and the unrenewed mind. This is the predesigned course of this world that he is following.

When we study chapter 5, we are going to discover that the believer who is out of fellowship imitates the unbeliever. A believer in this state cannot be led by his spirit or the Holy Spirit within him but will never be classified by God as a sinner. Because he is not controlled by his spirit at the moment, he is under the control of his flesh and his mind. He is imitating the unbeliever. Even though he may still go to church, give money, or act spiritual, his good deeds do not count with God. Sinners go to church, give money, and act spiritual to impress God into giving them a place in heaven. The believer who is not controlled by the Holy

Spirit at any moment in time is deceived and will act just like a worldly unbeliever.

"To be carnally minded is death; but to be spiritually minded is life and peace" (Romans 8:6.) When your mind is in line with your spirit, there is peace. When your mind is in line with your flesh, only things of death can be produced from your life. God calls the works resulting from these two conditions gold, silver, and precious stones (spiritual) or wood, hay, and stubble (carnal).

The unbeliever cannot be led by his spirit because it is dead—separated from the life of God—*"and were by nature the children of wrath."* The unbeliever does not need to change his deeds or his bad habits. He needs his nature changed. His problem is not his outward actions. Instead, it is the nature of his heart. The sinner is not a sinner because he sins. He sins because he is a sinner. The believer is not righteous because he does righteous acts. He does righteous acts because he is righteous. This should help us to straighten out our witnessing techniques. It is not up to us to make people feel guilty for their actions. God is not holding their sins against them. The reason they do not possess eternal life is because they have not accepted Jesus as their Savior.

They need their natures changed, and Jesus is the only One who can do this. Salvation is found in no other name than Jesus (Acts 4:12). Good works will not make us righteous, but righteousness will produce good works which are acceptable unto God. (See Ephesians 2:8–10.) We need to come right to the point with the sinner as Jesus did with Nicodemus: *"Ye must be born again"* (John 3:7).

In verses 1 through 3, we discover how God found us. In verse 1, we were spiritually dead. In verse 2, we were under Satan and his system. In verse 3, we were controlled by our fleshly nature and the unrenewed mind. In verse 4, we will come face to face with the love of God. Despite our condition, God loved us.

Now We're Born Again

Verse 4

But God, who is rich in mercy, for his great love wherewith he loved us.

I love the beginning of this verse, *"But God."* We were the subjects of the first three verses which describe how we were still a mess despite our good intentions and best efforts. *"But God!"* What a statement! God *"is rich in mercy."* The Greek word here is *plusios,* and it means "filthy rich." Pluto, whose name was derived from this word, was the god

of wealth in Greek mythology. This is also
where we get the English word *plutocrat*,
which is defined as someone who is so rich
that he has influence over other people. *"God,
who is rich in mercy,"* uses His wealth to influence us and win us over. God is rich in
mercy, which is grace in action. When grace is
displayed toward man, it is called mercy.
Mercy brings God's grace to lost man.

This principle is also seen in man. God has
given to each of His children the measure of
faith. Faith is the means of receiving God's
grace, but it does no good until it is put into
action. When faith is put into action, it is called
believing. Believing is faith in action. Faith
produces the ability within people to receive
the grace of God. God's grace always comes
first so that our faith has something to receive.
**Mercy is God reaching out to man, and be-
lieving is man reaching out to God.**

Maybe now you can begin to get a small
picture of the greatness of God's love to us.
Think of what He had to love—nothing! That
is why this verse says, *"for his great love
wherewith he loved us."* The love of God stag-
gers the imagination. *"For God so loved the
world that he gave..."* (John 3:16). Only God is
capable of so much love. Men occasionally
have displayed love beyond the ordinary. However, no man could ever love someone else the

way God loved and continues to love us. The
next verses amplify how great His mercy is.

Verses 5–6

*⁵ Even when we were dead in sins, [God]
hath quickened us together with Christ,
(by grace ye are saved;)*
*⁶ And hath raised us up together, and
made us sit together in heavenly places
in Christ Jesus.*

He loved us when there was nothing in us
to love. Remember, God did not love us because
of us, He loved us because of Himself. His love
not only found us; He cared enough for us not
to leave us in the condition in which He found
us. He gave us life and then raised us up out
of the mess and gave us a seat with Himself in
heaven. *"He raiseth up the poor out of the dust,
and lifteth up the beggar from the dunghill, to
set them among princes, and to make them inherit the throne of glory"* (1 Samuel 2:8).

I want you to notice all of the "togethers"
in verse 5: *"quickened us together…raised us
up together…made us sit together."* God per-
sonally could not come to redeem us because,
as a holy God, He could have no contact with
sin or with fallen man. He accomplished the
work of redemption through His Son. Jesus
became a man and took our place. *"The wages*

of sin is death" (Romans 6:23), but God could
not die to take our place. How would you kill
God, if He could die? How would you drive a
spear through God? How could you put nails
through Him or hang Him on a cross? The
only way God could take our place, our sin,
and our sicknesses was to become a man.

This also was part of the divine plan because God knew the work of the cross would
have to be substitution. God could not substitute for man. Man would have to substitute
for man. Jesus became sin for us in God's
place. Jesus died, went to hell, and rose again
for us in God's place. Since Jesus had no sin of
His own, God could raise Him from the dead.
We became identified with the work of Jesus
on the cross and in His death, burial, resurrection, and ascension.

I want you to get the picture. When God
found us, we were dead. He wanted us to be
alive and to sit with Him in His home, heaven.
Getting us from the point of death to a seat in
heaven with Him took the work of our mediator, Jesus. Since God could raise Jesus from
the dead, He could then bring us into heaven
to be seated with Him. Jesus could take hold
of us. When Jesus was raised from the dead,
we were raised up also. When Jesus ascended
to heaven, we ascended also. When Jesus was
seated in heaven, we were seated there too.

Jesus and all believers were made alive together, raised together, and made to sit in heavenly places together. *"For in Him we live and move and have our being"* (Acts 17:28).

Verse 7

That in the ages to come he might show the exceeding riches of his grace in his kindness toward us through Christ Jesus.

Why did God want us to sit in heavenly places with Him? He wanted us to be with Him throughout all eternity and share with Him all *"the exceeding riches of His grace."* He could not share eternity with us if we were not with Him. God not only has a plan for our lives here on earth after we are born again but also throughout all eternity. Just think, if God has a plan for us in eternity to come, He must plan on us making it past the few problems we face in life. You may be going through a hard time right now, and there doesn't seem any way out of it. However, God has a plan for you to get out of the mess, because He already has a place set for you in heaven for all eternity. If your future is secure, surely the present is also.

This verse also tells us something else. There is more grace waiting for us in heaven than we ever had in life. There is grace and *"more grace"* (James 4:6) available in this life. It is from that grace that God supplies our needs in life (Philippians 4:19). God has a vault of grace that has never been opened before. He calls it *"the exceeding riches of His grace."* This vault has enough grace to last throughout all *"the ages to come."* God's grace is inexhaustible.

Verses 8–9

[8] *For by grace are ye saved through faith; and that not of yourselves: it is the gift of God:*
[9] *Not of works, lest any man should boast.*

The Greek language is so unique that it has different tenses which can express the meaning of the sentence so well. The aorist tense is the regular past tense. The imperfect tense means that the action happened in the past again and again, a number of times at different intervals. Galatians 3:13 is in the aorist tense. *"Christ **hath redeemed** us from the curse of the law"*—once and for all.

In verse 8, *"saved"* is in the perfect tense, which combines the past (aorist) and the present tenses into one tense. Greek is the only language which has a perfect tense. The action takes place in the past, but the results continue up to the present time. Kenneth Wuest translates this verse better than anyone else I have found:

> 8 *For by the grace have you been saved in time past completely, through faith with the result that your salvation persists through present time.*[2]

When Jesus became the Lord of your life, eternal life was given to you. It has continued right up to the present moment. So, whether or not you feel like it or look like it, you are saved. You were saved in the past, and your eternal life continues. (See John 10:28.) That is the ongoing action of the perfect tense.

Grace and faith fit together. God's grace is received by our faith. Grace is God reaching out to us, and faith is our means of reaching out to Him. *"For by grace are you saved through faith; and that* [faith] *not of yourselves: it is the gift of God."* What is not of ourselves? The answer usually is that grace is not of ourselves, but that should be obvious. What this verse is really telling us is that faith is not of ourselves, it is the gift of God. Ephesians 3:12

---

[2] Kenneth S. Wuest, *The New Testament: An Expanded Translation* (Grand Rapids: Wm. B. Eerdmans, 1961), p. 451.

also tells us this: *"We have boldness and access with confidence by the faith of him."*

In Acts, we read about the crippled man's healing at the Gate Beautiful. Peter explained:

> *And his name though faith in his name hath made this man strong, whom ye see and know: yea, the faith which is by [from] him hath given him this perfect soundness in the presence of you all."*
>
> (Acts 3:16)

In Ephesians 2:9, Paul tells us that when it came to receiving the free gift of God—salvation—we did not even have the ability to become born again. God had to give us the ability to be able to receive His gift.

Imagine that the president of General Motors is your special friend. A new model car is to be placed on the market, and he has brought it by your house to show it to you before it ever hits the showroom floor. He is so excited that he wants to show it to you, his special friend, first. After he shows it to you and you realize how badly you want it, he tells you the price is $100,000. Then he asks why you are laughing! You are bankrupt and have no means of buying the car. Your friend tells you he has already placed in your bank account enough money to buy the car. In other words, he designed the car and then gave you the ability to purchase it.

Faith is not just our means of receiving salvation, but it is also our means of receiving anything else God has for us. Healing, finances, and freedom from worry and oppression are all available through the faith that God gives us. That way, all the glory goes to God the Father, not to us. If the faith came from us, we could boast before God. But since everything comes from God, even the means of attaining everything, then all the glory and praise goes to Him: *"Not of works* [human effort], *lest any man should boast* [glory in himself]."

In addition, we are not to worship the gift, but we are to reverence the Giver of the gift. Faith is a wonderful tool given to us to acquire all of God's blessings, but we should not worship faith. Many people today who are studying faith almost esteem faith as their god. All praise and glory should go to God and Jesus Christ. The Father is seeking those who will worship Him *"in spirit and in truth"* (John 4:23).

Verse 10

For we are his workmanship, created in Christ Jesus unto good works, which God hath before ordained that we should walk in them.

The Greek word for *"workmanship"* is *poema*. This is where we get the English word *poem*. It has to do with the special creation of God. We are God's special creation from His heart. When you read a beautiful poem, the glory doesn't go to the paper or pencil. The glory goes to the author, the creator of the work of art. We are God's creation. We are His workmanship. We are His masterpiece.

We are created *"unto good works."* You do not do good works to get saved. You are saved so that you can produce good works. Jesus Christ changed your nature on the inside. We were by nature the children of wrath. Good works do not produce a good nature. A good nature produces good works.

4

Jesus Removed the Barrier

Ephesians 2:11–22

In our discussion concerning the last half of the second chapter, we are going to be discussing the work of the cross in removing the barriers between God and man and between man and man.

The cross not only removed the barrier between God and man, it removed the barrier between races. There always has been and always will be racial prejudice in the world until Christ returns. People are going to be prejudiced because they are in Satan's world. The devil is the author of prejudice in the world. Since the cross, however, there is one place of true equality, and that is in Jesus Christ through the new birth. Galatians 3:28 states that in the body of Christ, there is no male or female (sexual distinctions), bond or free (social distinctions), nor Jew or Greek (racial distinctions). The Holy Spirit unites us all into one family through perfect love. We all have one Father who loves us all the same and gives us perfect love for each other.

Verse 11

Wherefore remember, that ye being in time past [before salvation] *Gentiles in the flesh, who are called Uncircumcision by that which is called the Circumcision in the flesh made by hands.*

This verse shows that races only exist in the flesh, not in the spirit. You were *"Gentiles in the flesh."* He also points out that those who called themselves *"the Circumcision"* (Jews) were not the true circumcision because they had only been circumcised in the flesh. The true circumcision consists of those who are born again and have been circumcised in the heart (Philippians 3:3). Notice the prejudice this verse reflects. Races always have slandered other races. Here, the Jews were calling the Gentiles *"Uncircumcision."* Those doing the name calling had missed the point.

Jews in the days of Jesus and Paul thought that physical circumcision caused a person to be acceptable to God. However, the rite of circumcision was designed by God, not to make them "acceptable," but to teach them of His plan. It was performed by the parents on the eighth day to remind them to teach the plan of God and separation from the world. Circumcision in the Old Testament was no different than water baptism today. The ritual does not save, but what it teaches can save. Racial barriers were removed on the cross by the work of Jesus at the same time that the sin barrier was removed through the shedding of His blood.

Verse 12

That at that time ye [Gentiles] were without Christ, being aliens from the commonwealth of Israel, and strangers from the covenants of promise, having no hope, and without God in the world.

Before we were born again, barriers existed between God and us and between the Jew and the Gentile. According to this verse, we were in a sorry condition. We were *"without Christ, aliens from the commonwealth of Israel, strangers from the covenants."* We had no

hope and were without God. We had a lot of
strikes against us. Let's begin to look at each
one of these conditions.

Aside from being "without Christ," we
were strangers *"from the commonwealth of
Israel."* Note that we were not strangers to
Israel, but rather we were alienated from the
"commonwealth." The commonwealth of Israel is the remnant within the nation who
were saved. The nation of Israel is a supernatural nation which was founded not on
natural generation but on regeneration. Abraham was not born a Jew; he was born a Gentile. What made him a Jew? Did circumcision
make Abraham a Jew? Did keeping a covenant
make Abraham a Jew? No, what made Abraham a Jew was his faith in the Lord. *"Abraham
believed God, and it was accounted to him for
righteousness"* (Galatians 3:6.) Faith turned
Abraham into the first Jew and the father of
us all. The nation of Israel has been a nation
since the time of Abraham, Isaac, and Jacob.
But just being born a physical Jew did not
mean these people were automatically God's
people. Faith makes us God's people.

Before we were born again, we were not
strangers to Israel, but we were *"aliens from
the commonwealth of Israel."* In other words,
we were disassociated from the righteous
remnant of the nation. God has always had a

remnant, according to the election of grace. There was, and is, a nation within the nation. Romans 9:6 tells us that not all Israel is Israel. This brings us back to the concept found in the opening verse of Ephesians that within a nation, a city, or church there is always a core of *"saints...and the faithful."* Now that we are born again, we are no longer *"aliens* [of another race] *from the commonwealth* [saved remnant] *of Israel."*

The Covenants of Promise

Next, we were *"strangers from the covenants of promise."* There are four covenants given to the nation of Israel. These promises are not for the entire nation. Instead, again they are for the commonwealth of Israel. These covenants will be fulfilled at the second advent of the Lord when Jesus comes to this earth to establish His millennial reign.

The first covenant is the Abrahamic Covenant. This referred to the Seed of Abraham (Jesus Christ) who would bless all nations through the faith of Abraham. God promised Abraham two sets of offspring in Genesis 12 and 15. Abraham was promised one set of offspring which would be as the sand of the sea. This would be a natural race called the Jewish nation. He was also promised a nation which

would number as the stars of heaven. This is
the spiritual offspring that would be the seed
of Abraham encompassing all nations on the
earth. Today the seed which is as the stars of
heaven is the church.

The second covenant is the Palestinian
Covenant. This was promised to Abraham
also, and it is the entire land which will one
day belong to the Jewish nation. Again, this is
not the nation just because they are physical
Jews but is made up of those who are born
again at the second coming of the Lord Jesus
to set up His kingdom on this earth. During
the reign of Solomon, Israel occupied the
greatest amount of land since the time of the
promise given to Abraham. The reign of
Solomon is a type of the millennial reign of
Jesus. But even during Solomon's reign, the
occupied land was nowhere near the size it
will be at the coming of the Lord Jesus as
King of Kings to rule on the earth.

The third covenant is the Davidic Covenant. This is found in 2 Samuel 7 and is God's
promise to David that he would have a son to
sit on his throne forever. To sit on the throne
of David, he would have to be a man from the
lineage of David. To rule forever, he would
have to be divine. There is only one who could
fulfill this promise, and that is Jesus. Notice
that this promise was given to the nation of

Israel—again, not to the physical nation, but rather to the spiritual commonwealth.

The last covenant is the New Covenant. This was given to us through the prophet Jeremiah who told of a covenant in which God would remove the heart of stone and put in its place a new heart of flesh. This is also a promise to the regenerate within the nation of Israel.

The verse in Ephesians that we are considering says that we were *"strangers from the covenants of promise."* What this verse is saying is that we were strangers when we were without Christ. So with Christ, we must not be strangers any longer to the covenants. Through faith in the Lord Jesus, we become righteous and a part of the Abrahamic covenant. *"And if ye be Christ's, then are ye Abraham's seed and heirs according to the promise"* (Galatians 3:29). We have a part in the Palestinian Covenant because we are promised that, during the millennial reign of Jesus, we will rule and reign with Him as He sits on His throne in Jerusalem. We have a part in the Davidic Covenant because Jesus is our King as well as the King to the nation of Israel. He is our spiritual King today and will be our physical King during His kingdom on this earth. We are a part of the New Covenant because our hearts have been changed from stony hearts into fleshly hearts through the work of the new birth. We are no longer strangers from the covenants of promise.

Verse 12 ends by telling us that we were without *"hope and without God in the world."* Thank God that with Jesus in our hearts, we now have a hope. Verse 18 of chapter one told us that we have a hope of our calling. We now have a hope in this life. No matter how bad this world may become, we know what the end will be. We have a hope in the soon return of Jesus Christ. We have a future with Jesus in His home, heaven. The sinner does not have a hope. He does not know what the future holds for him. If he did know, he would still have nothing to look forward to but an eternity in the lake of fire with the devil and his angels.

Without Christ, we also were *"without God in the world."* Now that we do have Christ, we also have God in this world. That is an astounding statement! We have God in this world. It is one thing to know that we will be with Him one of these days. It is another thing to know that He has come to be with us in this evil world. Right under the devil's nose and in his own world, God comes to live in us. He walks in us and guides us past the traps and snares that may lie ahead. We cannot fail. *"If God be for us, who can be against us?"* (Romans 8:31). No weapon formed against us shall prosper (Isaiah 54:17).

The Barrier Was Removed

Verse 13

But now in Christ Jesus ye who some-times [at one time] *were far off are made nigh* [near] *by the blood of Christ.*

The blood of Jesus Christ has brought me near to the Father. I was separated from God by an impassable gulf. God could have no fellowship with me, and I could have none with Him. Jesus came and removed the barrier between God and man.

Job described the barrier this way:

² *I know it is so of a truth: but how should man be just with God?*
³ *If he will contend with him, he cannot answer him one of a thousand.*

(Job 9:2–3)

God is infinite, awesome, holy, and righteous, and Job was just a man. He said that if God were to ask him 1,000 questions, he could not answer even one of them. The reason is brought out in Job 9:32–33:

³² *For he is not a man, as I am, that I should answer him, and we should come together in judgment.*

[33] *Neither is there any daysman* [medi-
ator] *betwixt us, that mighty lay his
hand upon us both.*

Job found the problem was that God was
not a man like himself. God is infinitely
higher than man. Job went on to wish for a
mediator who could come and join the two im-
possibilities together. If there were someone
who could lay one hand on God and the other
on man, he could unite them together. Well,
thank God there is! His name is Jesus Christ,
the God-man. He can satisfy the claims of
man because He is man. The work of the cross
united God and man together and brought us,
"who were [at one time] *far off...*[near] *by the
blood of Christ."* Jesus did all the work, and
we merely accept it. This means that all the
glory goes to Jesus who executed the plan and
God the Father who originated it. We can receive no glory at all.

Verse 14

*For he is our peace, who hath made
both one, and hath broken down the
middle wall of partition between us.*

Jesus is called *"our peace."* This is a reference to the ministry of reconciliation. Jesus
has made us reconciled to God.

> ¹⁷ *Therefore if any man be in Christ, he is a new creature: old things are passed away; behold, all things are become new.*
> ¹⁸ *And all things are of God, who hath reconciled us to himself by Jesus Christ, and hath given to us the ministry of reconciliation.*
> ¹⁹ *To wit that God was in Christ, reconciling the world unto himself, not imputing their trespasses unto them; and hath committed unto us the word of reconciliation.*
>
> (2 Corinthians 5:17–19)

The *"old things"* that have passed away are not cigarettes, beer, or chewing tobacco. They are the things associated with our old position before we were born again. We had no life because we were in Satan's kingdom, and we were spiritually dead. Now, after the new birth, *"all things are...new."* We now have spiritual life. We have a new position with Christ, seated with Him in heavenly places. We once were in the kingdom of darkness, and now we are in the kingdom of light. We were once in Adam; now we are in Christ.

It is true that we should have our lives clean before God, and unclean habits should be gone. But it should be because we are in Christ, in the family of God, and we should desire to walk as children of light. We do not give up bad habits to become saved. We become saved and now have the ability to put away the hindrances of the devil. Once you are born again, you have something to fill the void in your life and satisfy those cravings and desires. You now have the Word of God to feed your inner man, and you can fellowship with the Father through prayer and personal times of praise and worship.

> ¹⁸ *Who hath reconciled us* [past tense] *to himself by Jesus Christ, and hath* [past tense] *given to us the ministry of reconciliation;*
> ¹⁹ *To wit, that God was in Christ, reconciling the world unto himself.*
>
> (2 Corinthians 5:18-19)

He has not only reconciled us to Himself, He already has reconciled the whole world to Himself. The barrier between God and man has been removed. There used to be a barrier called "sin," but it is no longer the issue between God and man. There is no sin separating the sinner from God. Jesus was here on the earth *"not imputing the trespasses of men to them."* Jesus went to the cross and was judged for the sins of the world once and for all. Sins were judged on the cross. Jesus not only judged the acts and deeds of men, He condemned the very nature of sin in the flesh.

John the Baptist said of Jesus, *"Behold the lamb of God, which taketh away the sin of the world"* (John 1:29). If Jesus removed the sin of the world on the cross, then sin could not be the reason why men cannot go to heaven. The issue in salvation is no longer sin but Jesus. The question is not, What are you going to do about your sin? Rather, it is, What are you going to do with Jesus Christ? God made His move at the cross, and the next move is up to us. If the issue is still sin, then the issue is still too big for man to deal with. Man cannot do anything with his sin. If the issue is still sin, then why did Jesus have to come and die? What good was the cross? But since the issue is accepting Jesus or not, man can deal with that.

Even at the Great White Throne Judgment, the issue will not be sins but whether or not a person has accepted Jesus. *"And whosoever was not found written in the book of life was cast into the lake of fire"* (Revelation 20:15). Also, *"He that believeth on the Son hath everlasting life: and he that believeth not the Son shall not see life; but the wrath of God abideth on him"* (John 3:36).

Even though God has brought peace to the whole world, it is no good unless individuals accept it. Notice our verse again here in Ephesians 2:14, *"For he is our peace."* Peace has been provided for the whole world but is only made a reality through the new birth. It is one thing for Jesus to be the Prince of Peace. It is another thing for Him to be my Prince of Peace. True peace is a monopoly—for the believer only. To the unbeliever, peace is only potential. *"Therefore being justified by faith, we have peace with God through our Lord Jesus Christ"* (Romans 5:1).

Peace, like grace, can be multiplied as we learn more of God's Word. *"Grace and peace be multiplied unto you through the knowledge of God, and of Jesus our Lord"* (2 Peter 1:2). Peace is for and multiplied to the believer only.

You might ask, "But what about Luke 2:14? Didn't the angels announce, *'And on earth peace, good will toward men,'* at the birth of Jesus?" No, they didn't! If you look at other translations, you will find that the *King James Version* is misworded. The angels actually said, *"On earth peace among men with whom He is pleased"* (NAS). God is pleased with those who accept the Son He sent. He gives peace to those who become born again.

Peace is the message He has given us to proclaim. Just as Jesus came and preached peace, we have been given His message as ambassadors to give the word of reconciliation.

Our feet are declared to be beautiful because
we bring glad tidings of peace. (See Isaiah
52:7.) Our feet are *"shod with the preparation
of the gospel of peace"* (Ephesians 6:15). We
are called peacemakers because we bring men
into a place of right standing with God the
Father. (See Matthew 5:9.)

¹⁴ *For he is our peace, who hath made
both one, and hath broken down the
middle wall of partition between us.*

"Both one" refers to God and man, and
Jew and Gentile. God and man are now one,
and all races are now one in Christ. *"The
middle wall of partition"* is the barrier that
was between God and man and also between
the races on the earth. This barrier has been
removed by one act of reconciliation: Jesus'
death on the cross. True equality among races
only exists in the body of Christ. Only the
Holy Spirit can remove the prejudice placed in
the heart by Satan. It cannot be legislated
away or removed by man's will or desire but
only by the redemptive work of Jesus Christ.

Verse 15

*Having abolished in his flesh the en-
mity* [barrier], *even the law of commandments contained in ordinances;*

*for to make in himself of twain one new
man, so making peace.*

Jesus abolished the barrier. This means He
totally destroyed it. He did not bridge it over.
He totally wiped it out. Jesus abolished the
barrier in His flesh. This again shows the work
of His humanity on the cross. The cross was
sinless, spotless humanity dying for cursed, sinful humanity. The cross was total substitution.

"The law of commandments" refers to the
Ten Commandments. They are said in this
verse to be *"contained in ordinances."* This refers to the ordinances of feasts, fasts, sacrifices,
hygiene, Sabbaths, and so on. He abolished the
"commandments contained in the ordinances."
In Colossians 2:14, Paul says that Jesus
"blot[ted] *out the handwriting of ordinances*
[the law] *that was against us, which was contrary to us, and took it out of the way, nailing
it to his cross."* Jesus has removed us from the
curse of the law. The blessings are still intact
today. The blessings of Abraham come on the
Gentiles today through faith in Christ.

When Joshua took the people of Israel
into the Promised Land, he obeyed Moses' instructions in Deuteronomy 27 and 28 by taking them to two mountains and reading the
curses and blessings of the law. He read the
curses and half of the people who were on

Mount Ebal, said, "Amen." He read the
blessings, and the other half of the people
said, "Amen," from the other mountain
(Gerizim). After this, Joshua built an altar on
the cursing mountain, because redemption
was needed from the curses, not the blessings.
(See Joshua 8:30–35.) Now, we have been redeemed from the curse of the law, of which
the Ten Commandments are only a part.

Jesus said in Matthew 5:17, *"Think not
that I am come to destroy the law, or the
prophets: I am not come to destroy, but to fulfill."* Fulfill does not mean "to destroy." The
disciples would have loved for Jesus to do
away with the law so they would not have to
think of rules and regulations anymore. But
Jesus came to fulfill. Summer does not destroy
spring, it fulfills it. Manhood does not destroy
childhood, it fulfills it. However, once you are
a man, you shouldn't go back and act like a
child again. Likewise, now that you are in a
new dispensation, don't try to go back and live
under the law.

Paul pointed out to the Galatians:

> [3] *Having begun in the Spirit, are ye now
> made perfect by the flesh?...*
> [24] *Wherefore the law was our schoolmas-
> ter to bring us unto Christ, that we
> might be justified by faith.*

²⁵*But after that faith is come* [new birth],
we are no longer under a schoolmaster
[law].   (Galatians 3:3, 24–25)

*"For to make in himself of twain one new
man, so making peace."* God's purpose in removing the barrier was to make one new man,
the body of Christ. Through faith, we are all
part of one body, one church. As a result,
"making peace" shows that God's peace is a
monopoly for believers only. These believers
can be Jew or Gentile; white, black, red, or
yellow; male or female; bond or free. True
unity exists nowhere but in Christ.

Verse 16

*And that he might reconcile both unto
God in one body by the cross, having
slain* [abolished] *the enmity* [barrier]
thereby [by the cross].

The cross was the final fulfillment of the
law. Jesus fulfilled the sacrificial part of the
law when He went to the cross. He was the
perfect sacrifice. He fulfilled all the other
ordinances when He walked a perfect life on
this earth before His heavenly Father. On
the cross, when Jesus said, *"It is finished"*
(John 19:30), He was not referring to the

plan of salvation but to the Mosaic law. The law ended at the cross. Galatians 3:19 tells us that the law was added until the Seed should come. Jesus is the Seed of Abraham (Galatians 3:16). The law lasted from Moses until Jesus, the Seed. On the cross, Jesus removed the law by fulfilling it. He nailed it to the cross and abolished it. (See Colossians 2:14.)

Verses 17–18

¹⁷And came and preached peace [reconciliation] to you which were afar off, and to them that were nigh.
¹⁸For through him we both [those afar off and those near] have access by one Spirit unto the Father.

These are the *"twain"* of verse 15. *"You which were afar off"* are the Gentiles. *"Them that were nigh"* are the Jews. One group was a distance away, and the other one was near. The Jews were said to be near because of all the provisions they had in the Old Testament. God favored that nation of people. He gave them more revelation than anyone so they could take the message to the world—the Gentiles or the nations—those who *"were afar off."* But whether someone is far away or near,

he is still not in. The new birth saves a Gentile
and a Jew just the same. We both come in the
same way, *"by one Spirit unto the Father."*

Verses 19–20

> ¹⁹ *Now therefore ye are no more strang-*
> *ers* [noncitizens] *and foreigners* [one
> not at home], *but fellow-citizens with*
> *the saints, and of the household of God;*
> ²⁰ *And are built upon the foundation of*
> *the apostles and prophets, Jesus Christ*
> *himself being the chief corner stone.*

Jews and Gentiles are now *"fellow-
citizens."* We are all from one city, the heavenly Jerusalem, *"whose Builder and Maker is
God"* (Hebrews 11:10). Also, we are all, both
Jews and Gentiles, of the *"household of God."*
We are all members of the same family. We
can all claim God as our Father.

This verse goes on to tell us that we are
all (Jews and Gentiles) built on the same
foundation. That foundation is the Old Testament apostles and prophets. Isaiah not only
is the foundation for the Jew but also for the
Gentile. If we are both born again, we have
the same foundation. Jeremiah, Daniel, David,
and the rest of the Old Testament writers
have as much to say to me as to the Jews.

In the foundation, Jesus Christ is called *"the chief corner stone."* A chief cornerstone joins two walls together. Imagine two walls meeting at a 90-degree angle. At the bottom of the wall are the foundation stones. One stone is the cornerstone. Both walls meet in that one. The two walls here are a reference to the Old and New Covenants. What joins the two walls or covenants together is Jesus Christ.

The work of the cross went back in time as well as forward. The Old Testament saint was justified, or counted righteous, by looking forward to the work which was yet to come. We are justified by looking back to the work which already has been done. Isaiah said, *"We are healed"* (Isaiah 53:5), and 1 Peter 2:24 says, *"We were healed."* Jesus is the chief cornerstone. The other foundation stones are called apostles and prophets. Jesus is the chief apostle and the chief prophet. We are all *"living stones"* (1 Peter 2:5) built on the foundation of the Old and New Testament apostles and prophets of which Jesus is the chief cornerstone.

Verses 21–22

²¹ *In whom* [Jesus Christ] *all the building* [church] *fitly framed together groweth unto an holy temple in the Lord;*

²² *In whom ye also are builded together for
an habitation of God through the Spirit.*

In Acts 2:47, we find that *"daily"* the
church was growing. New believers are still
being added to the body of Christ each day. As
"living stones," we are all *"fitly framed
[joined] together [in]to an holy temple"* where
God can dwell. Even though we have different
personalities, natural origins, social positions,
or sexual distinctions, we are all joined together through the work of the Holy Spirit.

When Solomon built the temple, he had
the cedars fashioned in Lebanon and the
stones cut in quarries outside the city of Jerusalem. When the temple was finally assem-
bled, not a sound was made because each
stone and timber fit perfectly into the other.

⁷ *And the house, when it was in building, was built of stone made ready before it was brought thither: so that there
was neither hammer nor axe nor any
tool of iron heard in the house, while it
was in building.*   (1 Kings 6:7)

The world today does not know where we
came from or how we all work together. We
are a complete mystery to them. They keep
looking for some man-made organization or

program which brought us all together, a[...]
cannot be heard. The shaping of each stone [...]
done in private through the Holy Spirit and
the Word of God.

The temple in Solomon's day was built as
a house for God to live in through the presence of the Holy Spirit (the glory of God).
Verse 22 tells us that we also are *"builded
together for an habitation of God through the*
[presence of the Holy] *Spirit."* When Jesus
said on the cross, *"It is finished"* (John 19:30),
the veil of the temple was torn from the top to
the bottom so the presence of God could move
out of the stone temple into the hearts of His
new temple made of living stones. We are the
temple of God.

In this verse, we have the introduction of
the Holy Spirit, who is the main character in
the third chapter of Ephesians, which we will
study next.

5

A Look at the Mystery

Ephesians 3:1-12

The central character of chapter 3 of Ephesians is the Holy Spirit. God made the plan of redemption, as Paul relates in chapter 1. Jesus Christ executed the plan according to chapter 2. Now the Holy Spirit reveals it to mankind in chapter 3. This chapter will also define part of the plan of God that was reserved for the day in which we live—the church age. God had a plan in His heart that was not revealed until the time of the church, making our present time the most exciting time to live in that ever existed.

Verse 1

For this cause I Paul, the prisoner of Jesus Christ for you Gentiles.

"For this cause" is a reference to the end of the previous chapter where Paul is discussing the building up of the church, the temple of God. Because of the church and Paul's part in it, he is now a prisoner of the Lord. Although Paul is in a Roman prison, he does not call himself the prisoner of Nero or Caesar but *"the prisoner of Jesus Christ."* Even though he is in prison, the Lord is using him to bring this epistle to the believers in Ephesus. The apostle may be bound, but the gospel never is. The Word of God *"liveth and abideth forever"* (1 Peter 1:23).

Verse 2

If ye have heard of the dispensation of the grace of God which is given me to you-ward.

The Bible is divided into seven dispensations, the complete number of God. God is logical and organized despite the way many believers act or what they claim God told them. The Old Testament period covers five dispensations. *"God who at sundry* [different] *times and in divers* [different] *manners, spake in times past* [pre-Christ] *unto the fathers* [Jews] *by the prophets"* (Hebrews 1:1). In the Old Testament days, God spoke in different ways during different time periods. These time periods are the five dispensations from Adam to the cross of Jesus. The word for dispensation in the Greek is *oikonomia,* which means "a landlord" or "one who watches over a house." It may be better defined as "administration."

In our own country, we have administrations. When a new president is elected, he comes in with a new administration and usually dismisses many of the previous administration. God works in similar ways from one administration to the other. From dispensation to dispensation, many things change, yet many remain the same. How God speaks to man changes with the dispensation, but how man approaches God never changes.

God may approach man directly by walking and talking with him in the Garden of Eden, or He may teach him through angels as He did with Daniel and Ezekiel. Yet, during each time period, man has always approached God through faith. Hebrews 11 is a roster of God's Hall of Fame. Faith is the common thread running through each of the people listed, yet they cover every dispensation of the Old Testament. From Abel until the judges and prophets, God has said that *"without faith it is impossible to please Him"* (Hebrews 11:6).

Each of the five dispensations of the Old Testament begins with God's grace and ends with man's failure. The first dispensation began with the creation of Adam and Eve. It is called *innocence* and lasted until the fall. The second dispensation is called *conscience,* which ended with the flood in Noah's time. The third dispensation is *human government,* which ended with the building of the Tower of Babel. The fourth dispensation began with Abraham and is called *promise.* This period lasted until the Egyptian captivity when God raised up a deliverer for Israel named Moses. This marked the beginning of the final dispensation of the Old Testament called *law.*

We have previously discussed the law and said that it was given until the time of the crucifixion of Jesus. After the crucifixion, the door was opened for a new dispensation to be ushered in, which Paul calls in our passage, *"the dispensation of the grace of God."* This dispensation, which we call "the church age," began on the day of Pentecost and will end at the rapture of the church. During our dispensation, God approaches man in a unique way, but the way man approaches God is still the same as when Adam, Abraham, Moses, David, or any of the prophets approached Him—by faith. *"Hath in these last days* [the church age] *spoken unto* us [the church] *by His Son"* (Hebrews 1:2). The final dispensation will be the *millennial reign* of Jesus.

Paul also points out in this verse that the revelation of *"the dispensation of the grace of God"* was given to Paul to give to us—*"which is given me to you-ward."*

Verses 3–4

³ *How that by revelation he made known unto me the mystery; (as I wrote afore in few words,*
⁴ *Whereby, when ye read, ye may understand my knowledge in the mystery of Christ.)*

Paul has told them before of the revelation he received from the Lord about the doctrines of the church age.

¹¹ *But I certify you, brethren, that the gospel which was preached of me is not after man,*
¹² *For I neither received it of man, neither was I taught it, but by the revelation of Jesus Christ.*   (Galatians 1:11–12)

Now let's look at the word *"mystery."* This word comes from the Greek word *musterion* and refers to the teachings of ancient fraternities known only to its members. In the ancient world there were different fraternities, one of which is found in Matthew 2—the

Magi, or *"wise men."* This fraternal society of
men traveled in the regions of ancient Chal-
dea and Mesopotamia. Although their existence is well documented, their teachings and
beliefs are not. They were a secret organization whose creeds were called *"mysteries."* To
know and understand the teaching, you had to
become a member of the fraternity.

Fraternities still exist today, and the concept has never changed. To know the teachings and beliefs of such organizations as the
Masons or Odd Fellows, you have to become a
member. In no way am I endorsing these organizations for you to join but merely using
them as examples! Many such organizations
are satanic in origin, and their roots of operation go back to the ancient secret societies.

However, the word *"mystery"* is used re-
peatedly in the New Testament. Jesus first
used it with His disciples in Matthew 13:11 and
Mark 4:10–11. The kingdom parables, in which
Jesus was introducing the church age to come,
explained *"the mysteries of the kingdom."*

What is the significance of this word in
the New Testament? The prophets and saints
of the Old Testament did not know of the age
to come. Their concept of dispensations was
that, after Messiah came, the millennium
would be the next event on God's calendar.
This is why the disciples continually thought

that the kingdom was coming. The church was a *"mystery."* It was unknown to those on the outside looking in, but it is known to the members of the great fraternity known as the church. To know the teaching of the fraternity, you have to become a member.

The requirements for membership in the church are as follows:

> ⁹ *That if thou shalt confess with thy mouth the Lord Jesus, and shalt believe in thine heart that God hath raised him from the dead, thou shalt be saved.*
> ¹⁰ *For with the heart man believeth unto righteousness; and with the mouth confession is made unto salvation.*
>
> (Romans 10:9–10)

When you find the term *"mystery"* in the New Testament, it is not referring to something that is unknown to us. It is referring to something that was unknown but has been revealed to us.

Verses 5–6

> ⁵ *Which in other ages was not made known unto the sons of men, as it is now [the church age] revealed unto his holy apostles and prophets by the Spirit;*

⁶ *That the Gentiles should be fellow heirs, and of the same body, and partakers of his promise in Christ by the gospel.*

We see that in other generations it was not known, but it is now revealed. God has given us the revelation through the New Testament apostles and prophets, of which Paul is one. This revelation includes the fact that Gentiles can become born again and enjoy the blessings of the covenant. The barrier is removed through the work of Jesus on the cross.

Meat for Our Dispensation

The mystery includes the following points which are found in the New Testament epistles. It is meat for our dispensation only. They do not exist in the Old Testament.

1. *The individual priesthood of each believer.* Under the Old Covenant, only certain men were anointed to be priests. But today, you and I are individual priests before the Lord, our great High Priest (1 Peter 2:9).
2. *The infilling of the Holy Spirit.* This is for every believer. A few people were filled with the Spirit in the Old Testament, but it wasn't manifested by

speaking with tongues. The Holy Spirit would come on certain individuals and empower them (Luke 1:15), but now this is for every believer.

3. *The indwelling of the Holy Spirit.* When we believe on the Lord Jesus, the Holy Spirit comes and re-creates our spirit and makes it His new home. The Bible declares we are then the temple of the Holy Spirit (1 Corinthians 3:16). This is also something that did not exist in the Old Testament.

4. *The church.* The church did not begin until the day of Pentecost. Jesus prophesied, *"I will build my church, and the gates of hell shall not prevail against it"* (Matthew 16:18). When the last stone is placed in the church, it will be complete, and Jesus will come back for it. The church began on Pentecost and will end at the rapture.

5. *The body of Christ which is the church.* Not only are we members of His church universal, we are members of His body as individuals. The church eventually will become the bride of Christ when we are in heaven and have gone through the judgment seat of Christ.

6. *The gifts of the Holy Spirit.* There were supernatural   manifestations   all

through the Old Testament, but they were not for everyone. The three offices that were anointed by the Spirit were the prophet, priest, and king. Occasionally, other people were anointed but not everyone. Today, since every believer has the Spirit, every believer is told to *"covet"* spiritual gifts (1 Corinthians 12:31).

The teachings of the *"mystery"* include everything from Pentecost to the rapture of the church. Do you think the rapture could be part of the *"mystery"*? The answer is yes. Look at 1 Corinthians 15:51–52: *"Behold, I shew you a mystery; We shall not all sleep, but we shall all be changed. In a moment, in the twinkling of an eye..."* Here is a very important point. Teaching on the rapture of the church is found only in the epistles. You will not find the rapture depicted in the four Gospels or in the Old Testament.

When Jesus told about His coming in the Gospels, it was not a reference to the rapture but to the second advent and the ushering in of His millennial reign. (See Matthew 24.) At the rapture of the church, only believers will see Him. The rest of the world won't realize that anything has happened. But at the second advent of Christ, every eye shall see Him, *"every knee* [shall] *bow...and every tongue* [shall] *confess that Jesus Christ is Lord to the glory of God"* (Philippians 2:10–11). Here we have the major difference between the rapture of the church and the second advent of the Lord.

Let me give you some points that are not included in the mystery: the death and ascension of Jesus and His being seated at the right hand of the Father. Why would these not be included in the mystery? The reason is because they occurred before the day of Pentecost and are well documented in the Old Testament.

Let me give you three more points which are also not included in the mystery: the tribulation, the millennium, and the eternal state which occurs after the millennium. Why would these not be part of the mystery? Because all of these events occur after the church age is over. These all happen after the church is raptured and are also described in detail in the Old Testament.

Paul Completes the Deficiency

Again, I want to point out that Ephesians and Colossians are parallel. Therefore, let's look at an equivalent passage in Colossians 1:24–25:

> [24] *Who now rejoice in my sufferings for*
> *you, and fill up that which is behind of*
> *the afflictions of Christ in my flesh for*
> *his body's sake, which is the church:*
> [25] *Whereof* [for the church] *I am made a*
> *minister, according to the dispensation*
> *of God which is given to me for you, to*
> *fulfill* [complete] *the word of God.*

For the church, Paul was made a minister. Notice this: *"according to the dispensation of God."* That is the dispensation in which we live. *"Which is given to me for you, to fulfill the word of God."* How would you like to have the obligation on your shoulders to complete the Bible? It was up to Paul to fulfill or to complete the deficiency in the Word of God.

The Old Testament writers, all the way through the writing of the four Gospels, recorded the Word to a certain point. But the Lord gave Paul the responsibility of completing the deficiency. What is the deficiency that needed to be completed?

> [26] *Even the mystery which hath been hid*
> *from ages and from generations, but*
> *now is made manifest to his saints:*
> [27] *To whom God would make known what*
> *is the riches of the glory of this mystery*
> *among the Gentiles: which is Christ in*
> *you, the hope of glory.* (Colossians 1:26–27)

The mystery was the deficiency that needed to be fulfilled in the Word of God. Paul wrote most of the New Testament epistles. Now let's go back to Ephesians, chapter 3.

Verses 7–8

[7] *Whereof* [for the gospel] *I was made a minister, according to the gift of the grace of God* [apostleship] *given unto me by the effectual working of his power.*
[8] *Unto me, who am less than the least of all saints, is this grace* [apostleship] *given, that I should preach among the Gentiles the unsearchable riches of Christ.*

The word *"grace"* is mentioned many times in these verses and is a reference to the office of apostle in which Paul stood. He is actually setting up an introduction to the chapter to come where spiritual offices will be discussed for the body of Christ. Each one of these offices will also be called a *"grace"* (Ephesians 4:7). The reason they are each called a *"grace"* is because they are given by and energized by *"the effectual working of His power."* God is the giver and sustainer of each and every gift.

Paul also points out in verse eight that he considers himself to be *"less than the least of all saints."* This goes back also to the opening

verse of the epistle where he gives his name
and office. His name means "small" and his
office means "one of highest rank." The two
can go together when you realize that in the
natural you are nobody, but in the spiritual
you are somebody. Paul considers in this verse
that in the natural he is not worthy to be
given the office of an apostle.

When Paul was an unbeliever, he consid-
ered himself to be the chief of sinners (1
Timothy 1:15). In other words, he was on the
top of the ladder. Now, as a believer, he considers himself to be on the bottom, "less than
the least." I want you to understand that you
may have been the richest, most powerful, and
most famous sinner on the face of the earth
and are now the lowest member of the body of
Christ, but you still took a step up. The lowest
in God's kingdom is a promotion from the best
in Satan's. Paul is humbled to be given by God
the privilege of preaching *"among the Gentiles
the unsearchable riches of Christ."*

Take a lesson from what Paul is saying. If
you want to be used by God, don't try to promote yourself. If you have a choice between
taking the high road or the low road, take the
low one. You don't need to promote yourself
any more than David did as a shepherd. When
it was time to find a king, God knew where
David was, although Samuel did not. Men may

not know where you are, but God does. When David humbled himself, God promoted him.

"Humble yourselves therefore under the mighty hand of God, that he may exalt you in due time" (1 Peter 5:6). If you try to do God's job, He will have to do yours. If you try to exalt yourself, He will have to humble you. In the church that I pastor, it is amazing how many people want to preach from the pulpit but will not usher, teach class, or sweep the floor.

Jesus told His disciples that when they were invited to a wedding they should not take the upper seats because someone more prominent might come along and ask them to move down. He told them to take the lowest seat so the host might say to them, *"Friend, go up higher...For whosoever exalted himself shall be abased, and he that humbeleth himself shall be exalted"* (Luke 14:10–11). When you enter into ministry, start at the bottom. If you sense a call to the ministry but are not sure of the Lord's timing, start where you are. Find a Sunday school class to teach, a counseling position, or a maintenance job. Whatever you can find to do, do it with all your might.

By being faithful in the little things, you will be showing the Lord that He can trust you with larger responsibilities. One of these days, the Lord will reward you by saying, *"Well done, thou good and faithful servant:*

*thou hast been faithful over a few things, I will
make thee ruler over many things*" (Matthew
25:21). Operating in the lowest positions also
will help to create a servant's heart within
you which God will always use and promote.

Verse 9

*And to make all men see what is the fel-
lowship [dispensation] of the mystery,
which from the beginning of the world
[ages] hath been hid in God, who created all things by Jesus Christ.*

Before all the dispensations began, God
knew of the mystery. It may have been hidden
from men in Old Testament times, but nothing is hidden from God. Part of Paul's ministry
was not only to preach *"among the Gentiles
the unsearchable riches of Christ,"* but also to
make them see the importance of the time period in which they lived. Paul was commanded
by God to preach and reveal the mystery of
the church age for an important reason.

Verse 10

*To the intent that now unto the princi-
palities and powers in heavenly places
might be known by [through] the
church, the manifold wisdom of God.*

This verse will cause me to shout faster than any other. God doesn't come down and tell the devil how smart He is. He shows him how smart He is through us, the church. God had a secret from the foundation of the world, before all the ages began. After the fall of Lucifer, when evil was found in heaven and earth, God had a plan which was hidden in Himself for a day to come when every believer would be able to show on the earth *"the manifold wisdom of God."*

When Jesus arose from the dead, He gave all authority back to the church in His name. When a believer uses the name of Jesus, all hell comes to a halt. God is glorified, and the devil is humiliated. God smiles at Satan because we show forth His wisdom. We are inferior creatures to angels (Psalm 8:5; Hebrews 2:7) of whom Satan was the leader. We may be inferior by creation, but through the new birth we are superior by position. What is so humiliating to Satan is to be stopped through the authority in an inferior creature—man.

You cannot stop Satan in your own name, but you can in the name of Jesus. In the name of Jesus, you can cast out devils, speak with new tongues, and lay hands on the sick and see them recover. (See Mark 16:17–18.) That is the purpose of the mystery which was hidden in the heart of God. Can you now see why

it was so important for Paul to get this truth
across to the believers of his day and ours?

Verses 11–12

> [11] *According to the eternal purpose which*
> *he purposed in Christ Jesus our Lord:*
> [12] *In whom we have boldness and access*
> *with confidence by the faith of him.*

The mystery was planned between God
and the Lord Jesus in eternity past. This
takes us back to the counsel halls of eternity
(see the Ephesians 1 discussion) where God
planned the redemption of man before the
foundation of the world. Notice that verse 12
says that we have boldness and confidence in
Christ to approach the throne of God. We do
this through the *"faith of* [from] *him."* Again
we note that faith comes as a gift from God.
(See Acts 3:16; Ephesians 2:8.) The faith that
He gave us is our boldness and access to the
throne of God.

6

Paul Prays Again

Ephesians 3:13-21

Having told of our boldness to approach the throne of God through our faith, Paul now prays. This is his second prayer in this epistle. Both prayers come after Paul discusses God's plans which were set before the foundation of the world. In chapter 1, verses 15–23, Paul prayed his first prayer after telling us of all that God did for us in Christ in eternity past.

Here, he prays after telling us of God's foreknowledge in separating us as a special people to show forth His wisdom to the devil and his demons. The mystery was God's plan to give the church something that had never been given to believers before—individual authority over Satan for every member of the body of Christ. Being so overwhelmed, Paul could do nothing else but burst forth into a prayer for the revelation of the goodness and love of God the Father to become manifest in the heart of every believer.

Verse 13

Wherefore I desire that ye faint not at my tribulations for you, which is your glory.

Paul's introduction to the prayer is for the saints not to get their eyes on natural circumstances and faint. Fainting occurs in the mind when we get our eyes off the Lord and on other things in life or in people. Since Paul was in prison, the Ephesian saints might have a tendency to feel sorry for him and question God over his situation. Paul tells them not to become discouraged because God is getting glory while Paul is in prison.

God did not put Paul in prison. He is not that kind of God. Paul ended up in prison through his own mistake of disobedience. He desired to go up to Jerusalem and minister the Word in spite of warnings from God not to go. When Paul was thrown in prison, he eventually changed his attitude and repented, and God used the opportunity to turn cursing

into blessing. Paul told them that this was
for their glory. God always turns everything
to good when we trust Him. (See Romans
8:28.)

Verse 14

For this cause [their glory] *I bow my
knees unto the Father (of our Lord Jesus Christ).*

The reason I put the phrase *"of our Lord
Jesus Christ"* in parentheses is because it is
not found in many of the oldest manuscripts
or any of the better translations out today. It
is true that God is the Father of the Lord Jesus Christ, but that is not the subject. If the
phrase should be in there, it is an aside. We
are the subject, not Jesus. We are named after
the Father, not the Lord Jesus Christ.

Verse 15

Of whom [God the Father] *the whole
family in heaven and earth is named.*

Children are not named after the oldest
child but after their father. The *"family in
heaven* [and the family on] *earth is named"*
after God the Father. When you die and leave

this earth, you do not leave the family. You still are a part of the family of God. On this earth, we are a member of the family and of the church. At death, we leave the church but not the family. The church is also called the body of Christ. (See Colossians 1:18, 24.) We are all members of the body. When we die, we are no longer the eyes, hands, or feet because they are only needed on the earth. Someone is called by the Lord to fill in our place and fulfill the calling God has placed on our life. Never get the idea that your ministry is indispensable with the Lord. He got along fine before you came along, and He will do fine when you are gone. When significant ministers die, God doesn't die. They left the body and will be replaced, but they cannot and did not leave the family of God. The family exists in heaven and earth.

The rapture will be God's way of pulling the whole family together to be judged.

> [16] *For the Lord himself shall descend from heaven...the dead in Christ* [the family in heaven] *shall rise first:*
> [17] *Then we* [the family on earth] *which are alive and remain shall be caught up together with them in the clouds, to meet the Lord in the air.*
>   (1 Thessalonians 4:16–17)

Verse 16

That he [the Father of the family] *would grant you, according to the riches of his glory, to be strengthened with might by his Spirit in the inner man.*

The word *"strengthened"* is the Greek word *kratos* which means ".ruling power." God wants you to have ruling power in your inner man. This is the ability to channel and direct your life through the pressures and obstacles that Satan and the world may bring. We are kings in life, but often we do not know how to properly rule our own lives, let alone give anyone else help with theirs. We rule *"with might."* The Greek word for *"might"* is *dunamis*. This means "inherent power," and is a reference to your faith. Your faith is the power by which you rule. By using the faith God has given you, you become stabilized in life. Circumstances no longer dictate to you. You dictate to them. You become the master over the affairs of life, and you truly can reign in life as a king.

Verse 17

That Christ may dwell [be at home] *in your hearts by faith; that ye, being rooted and grounded in love.*

It is one thing for the Lord to live in your heart; it is another thing for Him to feel at home. When you begin to rule in life through the faith He has placed in you, then Christ feels at home in you. However, this verse tells us not only that we need to operate in faith and be strengthened with might, but also we need for our lives to be *"rooted and grounded in* [God's] *love."* Love is a foundation of our lives because faith is useless without love. *"Faith...worketh by love"* (Galatians 5:6). What nullifies faith is fear. Fear is the opposing force to faith. What keeps fear away is love. *"Perfect love casteth out fear"* (1 John 4:18). This is why faith and love go hand in hand. Love keeps the fear away and lets the faith operate.

Verse 18

May be able to comprehend with all saints what is the breadth, and length, and depth, and height.

You are not a one-man band. God has not called you to be a maverick in the body of Christ. Everybody can and should accomplish the plan of God together as a team. No matter what revelations you have from the Word of God and from the Holy Spirit, you should be ready and open to share them with other believers. God's desire is for all the body to grow at the same rate. What would your body be like if the hand grew faster than the rest of your body? You would be a freak. God wants us *"to comprehend with all saints."*

Once you have been rooted and grounded, the Lord's desire is for you to grow by comprehending and learning His Word. This is what is meant by *"breadth, and length, and depth, and height."* The word *"breadth"* in the Greek means "storage space." It refers to all the categories of the Word of God. Do not become one who gets off on a tangent. Go for the entire width of the Word of God. Don't get hung up on one subject and see it as the only subject which pleases God. Many people discover one key component of the Christian life and immediately make it a panacea for every problem. They are always looking for the one key that will fit all locks.

Jesus did not say, *"I will give unto thee the key of the kingdom,"* but *"the keys"* (Matthew 16:19). The wise man knows which key to use for the proper door. Prayer is important, but it is not the only key to the Christian life. Praise, worship, study, deliverance, confession of God's promises, and speaking with other tongues all are important, too. But none of these alone will sustain you and give you victory. You need to be balanced in all areas of your life. These are all keys the Lord has given to us to use at the proper time. This is *"the breadth"* we are to comprehend.

"Length" has to do with time orientation, with knowing where you are on God's dispensational calendar. Remember our teaching on the mystery at the beginning of Ephesians 3? Each dispensation is important and should be studied, but one is more important to us than all the others—the church age. The majority of your study should be in the New Testament epistles because this is meat for our time: *"...and be established in the present* [church age] *truth"* (2 Peter 1:12).

"Height" refers to your attitude toward God, and *"depth"* to your attitude toward men. One is vertical (height) and the other horizontal (depth).

> *Thou shalt love the Lord thy God* [height] *with all thy heart, and with all thy soul, and with all thy strength, and with all thy mind; and thy neighbor* [depth] *as thyself.*   (Luke 10:27)

Let's review what we have discussed about this passage. After you become rooted and grounded in love, operating in faith, God wants you to mature in these dimensions:

1. All areas of the Christian life.
2. The part of the Word for our time period, the church age.
3. Your love relationship with Father God.
4. Your love relationship with your fellow believers in the body of Christ.

Verse 19

And to know the love of Christ, which passeth knowledge, that ye might be filled with all the fullness of God.

God always sets high goals. He tells you to be holy as He is holy (1 Peter 1:16), to sin not (1 John 2:1), and to imitate God (Ephesians 5:1). These sound like tall demands, and they are. But thank God He has given us the Holy Spirit to live in us and live out His life through us. If God says I can know the love of Christ, then I can. It might stagger the imagination, but I will say with Mary, *"Be it unto me according to thy word"* (Luke 1:38).

I believe that by looking at this verse we can see that we have a lifetime job ahead of us. As I grow each day, my goal is to be just like God in this world. I want people to look at me and see the Lord. Many people may never come to church, pick up the Bible, turn on a television, or listen to a radio broadcast. But

they can see me. Jesus gave me the Holy
Spirit to be a witness. (See Acts 1:8.)

Verse 19 tells us that the love of Christ
"passes knowledge." The Greek word for
"knowledge" is *gnosis.* It is a reference to
man's knowledge. God's love surpasses anything man knows. People may be able to argue
your doctrine, but they stand speechless in the
presence of divine love.

Verse 20

> *Now unto him that is able to do exceed-
> ing abundantly above all that we ask or
> think, according to the power that
> worketh in us.*

The word for *"power"* in this verse is our
old friend *dunamis.* We found it in verse 16,
and it referred to our faith. Faith is the power
God has put in us to reign in life and now to
receive answers to prayer.

"Worketh" refers to the use or exercising
of your faith. When your faith is being used in
prayer, God is able to answer your prayer and
not only that but to *"do exceeding abundantly
above all that we ask or think."*

If God did more than I could ask, that
would be big in itself. But when He adds
"think" to it, it becomes staggering. I can ask

for some big things, and I also can think of things that are more than I dare ask for. When I use the faith I have, God not only answers that, but goes an extra step and gives things I could only imagine.

Have you ever thought of something you would like in life but never really took the time to ask for it? Has God brought those things to you anyway? Of course He has. This has happened to me more times than I can count. He is a loving heavenly Father. I would do the same thing for my son. If I even hear him mention something he would like, I do my best to get it for him. *"If ye then, being evil [natural], know how to give good gifts to your children, how much more shall your Father which is in heaven give good things to them that ask him?"* (Matthew 7:11).

Verse 21

Unto him [God] be glory in the church by Christ Jesus throughout all ages, world without end. Amen.

God, who is the author of the plan, sent His own Son to the cross to redeem us and gave us the Holy Spirit to reveal His plan to us. He is the One who receives all the praise, from now and forever.

Notice that in this verse God's desire is to receive glory *"in the church."* Individual praise is good. However, just as He wants the whole church to mature (v. 18), He wants the whole church to glorify Him. This is not only something for the time we are on earth but also through all of eternity.

Many people do not like worship and praise because they feel foolish in the congregation raising their hands, clapping, singing loudly, and dancing. They should get used to this type of praise because it will be this way throughout all eternity, forever and ever. Why wait until you go to heaven to please God? Try it right now. We live our lives and use our mouths to give God glory (Colossians 3:17).

Beginning in Ephesians, chapter 4, we come to the transitional point of the book. We will shift from positional truth (who we are in Christ) to temporal truth (the daily life of faith). Now that we know we are righteous, holy, redeemed, and seated with the Lord in heaven, we need to use this wisdom in our everyday lives. The *"righteousness of God"* must still wash dishes, go to work, raise children, maintain a marriage, and get along with the boss. Practical application of the Word is the subject of the last half of Ephesians.

7

The Unifying of the Body

Ephesians 4:1-16

In chapter 4, we begin the application part of the book. If we were to end the book right here, we would have tremendous truths but no practical wisdom at all. As we noted earlier, chapters 1 through 3 of Ephesians contain positional truth—who we are in Christ. The second half of the book, chapters 4 through 6, contains practical or temporal truth. Temporal truth is the application of positional truth to our everyday lives. Because I am righteous, now I can live it. Because I am holy, now I can be holy. Because I am sanctified, now I can act sanctified.

One of the keys for us to make the transition from positional truth to temporal truth is the use of the baptism in the Holy Spirit. This will come up in the next chapter. The baptism in the Holy Spirit is given to us to help bring our natural lives into a place to show others the Lord in us. Jesus said the Holy Spirit was given to us to help us *"be witnesses"* (Acts 1:8). The main use of the Holy Spirit is not just to help us speak in tongues but also to help us be witnesses on the job, in the home, in school, or anywhere we might be.

In the first three chapters, we have been gaining knowledge. In studying the last half of the book, we will be applying that knowledge in the form of wisdom. **Wisdom is the correct application of knowledge.** We have been hearers of the Word; now we will become doers. (See James 1:22.)

The first three chapters give strength to the inward man. Now the inward man is going to be given something on which to use that strength—being sanctified. Sanctification is the theme of the last half of chapter 4 and the first half of chapter 5.

The things Paul tells us to do in the last half of Ephesians are impossible for the natural man to do in his own strength. Living the Christian life is impossible. Only when the power of the Lord is used can the Christian

life become a reality. Through the Word and
the infilling of the Holy Spirit, we can live the
life of Christ in the devil's world.

Verse 1

*I therefore, the prisoner of the Lord, be-
seech you that ye walk worthy of the vocation wherewith ye are called.*

The word *"walk"* indicates that we have
moved from positional to temporal truth.
Positionally, we are seated with the Lord
(Ephesians 1:20; 2:6). Temporally, we are
walking. Walking is an outward physical
function which represents a spiritual truth.
Just as walking in the natural is a means of
traveling from one place to another, in the
spiritual, walking refers to traveling from
immaturity to spiritual adulthood. Walking
requires one step at a time, just as the Christian life is lived one day at a time. (See Matthew 6:34.) Spiritual maturity takes many
steps, but all must be taken one at a time,
*"precept upon precept; line upon line...here a
little, and there a little"* (Isaiah 28:10).

There are nine areas or spheres about the
Christian walk listed in the New Testament.
Each of them requires putting our knowledge
of the Word of God into daily operation in our

lives. The first area of our walk is in the Word of God. We are told to walk in the truth that is in us in 3 John 3. The second area of our walk is in the Holy Spirit, in order to overcome the temptations of the flesh. Galatians 5:16 tells us to walk in the Spirit, and Romans 8:4 tells us to walk not after the flesh. The third area of our walk is in faith: *"We walk by faith, not by sight* [senses]" (2 Corinthians 5:7).

The fourth area is our love walk before the Lord. Ephesians 5:2 tells us to walk in love. The fifth sphere of our walk is in newness of life. This outward display of our changed life is found in Romans 6:4. The sixth area is our walk of integrity before the world. Christians should be the most dependable people in the world. Romans 13:13 tells us to *"walk honestly."* The seventh area of our walk is in our spiritual production, or fruit-bearing. This is found in Ephesians 2:10 where we find that God wills for us to walk in good works. The eighth area of our walk is in our calling, or the ministry office in which we stand. This is the subject of the passage in Ephesians 4:1: *"Walk worthy of the vocation wherewith ye are called."* The ninth area involves our walk before unbelievers in the world. Colossians 4:5 tells us to *"walk in wisdom toward them that are without." "The steps of a good man are ordered by the Lord"* (Psalm 37:23).

Verse 2

With all lowliness and meekness, with longsuffering, forbearing one another in love.

"Meekness" is a "teachable attitude." A meek person is not a doormat or a weak person but someone who has a teachable spirit. James tells us to *"receive with meekness the engrafted word"* (James 1:21). In Matthew 5:5 Jesus says that the meek will inherit the earth. Meek, or teachable, people are well rewarded in this lifetime and in eternity to come. Never come to a place in your Christian walk where you think you know it all. Until we come into heaven with the Lord, we will always be learning. If you think you can be taught no more, then you have just admitted your ignorance. The more you learn in this life, the more you find out you do not know.

The word *"longsuffering"* here means "patience." It is the same word translated *"patience"* in Hebrews 6:12, where it is stated that we are to be *"followers of them who through faith and patience inherit the promises."* We all need patience in this life because it is a partner to the successful life of faith.

The word *"forbearing"* is beautiful in the Greek. It means "to stand one's ground."

You can be teachable and patient, and yet stand your ground with other believers. We do this *"in love."* Sometimes you need to stand your ground for something you know is right, but you always should do it in an attitude of love.

I envision someone who is immovable in love when I read the way David describes a righteous person as a *"tree planted by the rivers of water"* (Psalm 1:3). These trees are the strongest because they always have a constant source of water. They also outlive other trees because they have no fear of drought. A strong tree bends in the wind but is never uprooted. As believers, we are trees planted by streams of living water. We are not rigid but bendable. You have to listen to what other people say and weigh it in your own spirit. At times you may change your own mind; other times you may not. You have to stand for the truth, but you must do so in a manner of love, *"forbearing one another in love."*

Verse 3

Endeavoring to keep the unity of the Spirit, in the bond of peace.

Many Christians confuse our mission in life. They believe God has left us here to agree in our beliefs and doctrines. This will not occur until we are in heaven. This will be found later in verse 13 with *"the unity of the faith."* This will be accomplished by Jesus Himself after the judgment seat of Christ. Our purpose as believers is to keep *"the unity of the Spirit."* This is harmony over our mission, not our beliefs. Our mission is the Great Commission as given in Matthew 28:19–20 and Mark 16:15–18. We will never agree on all doctrines, but we can get along with each other in peace while we win others to Jesus. This type of unity is not as easy as it sounds.

Notice that we are to endeavor to keep the unity of the Spirit. The Greek word for "endeavoring" is *spoudazo*. This word means to be diligent or work hard. Maintaining unity among people of diverse beliefs and backgrounds is hard work. Without the Holy Spirit, it would be impossible. With the Holy Spirit, our hard work will pay off.

The Body as One

Verses 4 through 6 are going to tell us everything that we have in common—seven factors which unify all believers. The main personality in verse 4 is the Holy Spirit. In verse 5, the main personality is Jesus Christ. In verse 6, the main personality is God the

Father. Each of the members of the Godhead has a specific part in the unifying of the body of Christ. The Holy Spirit makes us all one body. The Lord gives us all one faith. The Father unifies us by being in us all.

Verses 7 through 11 are going to tell us what we all have as individuals. I am glad that I am a member of the body of Christ, a part of the whole, yet I am still an individual. God loves me the same as He loves everyone else in the body of Christ, but He rewards me as an individual.

Verse 4

There is one body, and one Spirit, even as ye are called in one hope of your calling.

The *"one body"* is the body of Christ talked about in 1 Corinthians 12:13: *"For by one Spirit are we all baptized into one body."* At the moment of the new birth, the Holy Spirit plunges us into the body of Christ. Although there are many local bodies or local churches we may attend, there is one universal body, the church of the Lord Jesus Christ.

We also have *"one hope of our calling."* Something else which unifies all believers is the knowledge that Jesus is coming back for all of us to take us to heaven to be with Him forever. This is the great hope of the church. (See 1 Thessalonians 4:13 and 1 John 3:3.)

Verse 5

One Lord, one faith, one baptism.

There is only *"one Lord"* and Redeemer, the Lord Jesus Christ. We all look to one Head of the church who earned that position by His death, burial, resurrection, ascension, and seating at the right hand of God the Father. He is King of Kings and Lord of Lords.

There is also *"one faith"* which makes us all members of one body and gives us one Lord. This is the measure of faith by which we are born again (Ephesians 2:8). This faith can grow through knowledge of God's Word (Romans 10:17) and can bring us many more blessings in this life. You really never gain more faith but grow and increase in the *"one faith."*

The *"one baptism"* is not water baptism. This again is the baptism of the new birth found in 1 Corinthians 12:13:

> *For by one Spirit are we all baptized into one body, whether we be Jews or Gentiles, whether we be bond or free; and have been all made to drink into one Spirit.*

There is only one baptism which makes us members of one body, gives us one Spirit, gives us one hope of our calling, gives us one Lord, and delivers us one faith.

Verse 6

One God and Father of all, who is above all, and through all, and in you all.

Christianity is not like religions around the world that have many gods. We have one God, who is the *"Father of all"* who have made Jesus their Lord and Savior. He is said to be *"above all."* He is the highest in rank because He is even the Father of our Lord Jesus. All majesty, power, dominion, praise, and worship goes to Him. There will even come a day when all of Satan's kingdom will admit that He is above all, including them. (See Philippians 2:10–11.)

God is said to be *"through all."* This means that God is infused in everything. He is a part of all creation whether it is heavenly, earthly, spiritual, or natural. Even the sinner was created by God and will one day admit to that. Finally, God is *"in you all."* Notice that God is above and through all—believer and unbeliever alike. But He is only *"in"* the believer. He is *"in you* [the saints at Ephesus] *all."* The teaching that God lives in everyone is wrong. He only lives in those who make His Son their Lord and Savior.

Believers as Individuals

Now we come into what each believer has as an individual.

Verse 7

But unto every [each] *one of us is given grace according to the measure of the gift of Christ.*

Each one of us has been given grace by the Lord Jesus. Grace is a reference to the ministry office in which we stand. The offices all are extensions of Jesus Himself. Jesus is the evangelist, the apostle, the teacher, the pastor, and the prophet. All of the offices in which we stand as servants of Christ are manifestations of the different ministries of Christ. These offices are called "graces" because they are not of our own choosing or works. Each person's calling is a gift of God. You will never be happy in your Christian life until you discover and accept your calling. You cannot fulfill what someone else is called to do. Stop being jealous of someone else's calling

and spiritual gifts and realize that God has
called you to be unique. Your gifts and callings
cannot be fulfilled by someone else. The body
of Christ is a team, and we all need to play our
parts.

Verse 7 is an introduction to the five
ministry offices of verse 11: apostle, prophet,
evangelist, pastor-teacher. These are the
"pulpit" offices, or offices of those who instruct congregations. But these are not the
only offices listed in the Word of God. There
are twelve offices all together found in the
New Testament which comprise the entire
body of Christ. Besides the five listed here in
Ephesians 4 and 1 Corinthians 12:28, the
other seven are found in Romans 12 which are
the "body" offices. Every member of the body
of Christ stands in an office whether they ever
stand in a pulpit or not.

Paul begins to instruct concerning the
seven body offices in Romans 12:3 by explain-
ing, *"For I say, through the grace given unto
me."* The grace given to Paul was the office of
the apostle. Paul was speaking here through
his apostolic office to the saints at Rome telling them not to be high-minded toward other
believers. *"For as we have many members in
one body, and all members have not the same
office"* (v. 4). Each of us have an office but not
the same office. *"Having then gifts differing*

according to the grace [office] *that is given to us"* (v. 6). We all have a ministry office just like Paul, Peter, James, or any of the others listed in the New Testament.

In Romans 12:6–8, Paul goes on to list the seven offices found in the body of Christ. These offices begin with *"prophecy"* (v. 6). This is very similar to the office of the prophet found in our passage in Ephesians 4:11. Every prophet began by giving prophecies, but because a person gives a prophecy does not mean that he is a prophet.

The next office listed is *"ministry"* (v. 7). The Greek word here is *diakonos* from which we derive the English word "deacon." I want you to notice that a deacon is not a fivefold minister. He is a member of the congregation and is not set in the church to run the pastor, who is a fivefold minister. When a deacon proves himself faithful, he can *"purchase…a good degree* [promotion]" (1 Timothy 3:13) for himself.

A deacon is a server. There are many people in our churches who feel called to serve others. These make the best ushers, communion servers, maintenance people, and workers. They are motivated to do these jobs because this is their calling in the body of Christ. We should not put people into jobs in the church on our own whim, but we should wait for their

calling to become evident to us so we can place
them in the positions which are most effective
for the church and their own lives.

The next office is the teacher (v. 7). This
again is not the fivefold ministry office of the
teacher but one who is *"apt* [suited] *to teach"*
(2 Timothy 2:24). There are many people in
the church who are fitted to teach and may
never stand in the pulpit ministry of a
teacher. But one thing is for sure, the fivefold
teacher did not begin without being *"apt to
teach."* The desire to teach has been in his
spirit for a long time. When a person proves
himself faithful to teach, God can use that as
a point of promotion into the fivefold teaching
position.

The fourth office mentioned is the exhorter (v. 8). This person may not be apt to
teach, but he has a God-given ability to encourage and exhort sinners to become born
again or believers to become more dedicated to
the Lord. These people love to counsel others
and to encourage people one-on-one. The exhorter also loves to witness and seems to have
a God-given gift of winning people to the
Lord. We are all called on by the Lord to witness (Mark 16:15), but the exhorter has a gift
in this area. I find that the exhorter is usually
the one called on by the Lord to later fulfill
the fivefold office of the evangelist.

The next office listed is the giver (v. 8). Stewardship is something taught throughout the Old and New Testaments to all believers. There are some called by God though to stand in the body office of the giver. This person is motivated to give by a call in his heart. This person does not give to be noticed, but rather he does it *"with simplicity* [not for outward show]." We are all told that we can prosper in life by giving into the kingdom of the Lord. However, the giver is prospered by God above the ordinary in his business and personal finances because of the calling on his life to put large sums of money into the spreading of the gospel message.

The sixth office is the ruler (v. 8). These are the elders, the ones who help in the church in the area of pastoral care. In 1 Timothy 3:2–4 we find that the two qualifications for the elder in the Word are that he rule and teach. Notice that this office also is not a fivefold office as is that of pastor. Elders are not to run the church but work in cooperation with the pastor in the care of the people. A "body" office is not to run the fivefold offices which Jesus chooses and places in the church. The ruler is the one God usually calls on later to fulfill the office of the pastor.

Remember that these offices listed in Romans 12 are offices found within the body of Christ and are still sheep to be watched over by the shepherd (pastor). The sheep never run the shepherd. The older sheep (elders) can help when the shepherd oversees the other sheep but never usurp his authority. It takes a miracle to turn a sheep into a shepherd, and that is exactly what happens when God puts the call on a faithful member of the congregation to step into a fivefold ministry office.

The last office listed is that of the mercy giver (v. 8). This person takes the hurts of others on himself and displays the mercy of God and compassion toward the unbeliever, the sick, and the hurting. These people love to visit those in hospitals, nursing homes, and jails. We are all called to love each other and show the mercy and compassion of God, but some are gifted specifically by God in these areas.

I think you can see that we each have all the areas involved in the offices represented in our lives, but one or more of them take priority. God magnifies these areas in each person's life after he becomes born again. When a pastor and other church leaders begin to wait on the Lord for these offices to become magnified in the lives of the members, then the needs of the church will be fulfilled by those called to specific positions.

"But unto each one of us is given grace [a ministry office] *according to the measure of the gift of Christ."* The next verse now begins to describe some of those offices which take authority in the body of Christ, the fivefold ministries.

Verse 8

Wherefore he saith, When he ascended up on high, he led captivity captive, and gave gifts unto men.

This verse is a quotation of Psalm 68:18. It reinforces what we learned in Ephesians 3:14–15 that there are two ranks in the family of God: *"For this cause I bow my knees unto the Father...of whom the whole family in heaven and earth is named."* Part of the family is in heaven; the other part is on the earth.

When Jesus ascended up on high, He didn't give gifts to part of the family and not to the rest. The captivity He led captive is the family which is now in heaven, and the gifts He gave to men is the family on earth.

At the time of the crucifixion, believers from the Old Testament age had not yet gone to heaven to the presence of the Father. They went underground to a compartment called paradise or *"Abraham's bosom"* (Luke 16:22). They waited there for the time of redemption

when Jesus would come and take them into
the presence of God in heaven. At the ascension of Jesus, this group of people went up
with Him as He freed them. An interesting
thing happened at the resurrection of the
Lord: Jesus received a resurrection body; and
many of the Old Testament saints received
their old bodies back and came out of their
graves, went into Jerusalem, and appeared to
many of the people there. (See Matthew
27:52–53.) These people, like Lazarus, eventually died again but then went directly into
the presence of God in heaven. Jesus is the
only one right now with a resurrection body.
We will all receive ours at the great resurrection, the rapture of the church. (See 1 Thessalonians 4:16–17 and 1 Corinthians 15:51–53.)

The gifts that the Lord gave to men will
be listed in verse 11, which are the fivefold
ministries. Verses 9 and 10 are parenthetical
to describe who led captivity captive and gave
the gifts to men. Verse 11 will take up where
verse 8 left off and describe the gifts given.

Verse 9

Now that [expression], *he ascended,
what is it* [what does it mean] *but that
he also descended first into the lower
parts of the earth?*

Notice that this verse tells us that Jesus went into the lower parts of the earth. This is plural because Jesus went into all the parts. Jesus told us in Matthew 12:40 that no sign would be given to that generation except the sign of the prophet Jonah:

> [40] *For as Jonas was three days and three nights in the whale's belly; so shall the Son of man be three days and three nights in the heart of the earth.*

Jesus descended *"into the lower parts of the earth."* After Jesus died on the cross, He went into the regions of the lost as the scapegoat went into the wilderness. (See Leviticus 16:20–22.) To find some interesting types of what happened to Jesus in the lower parts of the earth, read Jonah, chapter 2. What Jonah experienced in the whale's belly is what Jesus experienced in *"the lower parts of the earth."*

Verse 10

He that descended is the same also that ascended up far above all heavens, that he might fill [complete] *all things.*

Just as *"parts"* is plural in verse 9, so is *"heavens"* in verse 10. Scripture refers to three different heavens. Jesus went through all of them on His way to the right hand of the Father. The first heaven surrounds the earth, and we know it as the atmosphere. The second heaven is the area of the stars, moon, and planets, known as space. The final heaven is the abode of God Himself, the third heaven. This is where the saints went at the ascension of Jesus and where believers go today when they die. This is also the place where Paul went in 2 Corinthians 12:4, and where John went in the book of Revelation.

Jesus went to heaven so *"that He might* [complete] *all things."* The plan of redemption was not completed until Jesus sat down at the right hand of God the Father. Jesus sat down because the plan was over. He had completed His work. God rested on the seventh day of creation not because He was tired but because the work was completed. Jesus completed the plan of redemption when He arrived in heaven and sat down until the day of His return to begin the millennial reign, the day when His enemies will be made His footstool (Hebrews 1:13). The plan of redemption is complete. All that remains now is the final enforcement of that victory when Satan and his demons will be consigned to the bottomless pit for 1,000 years during the reign of Jesus on the earth (Revelation 20:1–3).

Verse 11

And he gave some, apostles; and some, prophets; and some, evangelists; and some, pastors and teachers.

The *"He"* that gave the gifts is the Lord Jesus, the one who descended, ascended, and completed all things. In 1 Corinthians 12:28, we find that He gave these gifts to the church. As long as we still have the church, we still have all five of the ministry offices. In chapter 1, we discussed the ministry office of the apostle. Some people think we no longer have apostles or prophets today. But Jesus put them *"in the church."* Since we still have the church, we still have apostles and prophets, along with evangelists, pastors and teachers.

It is not my intention to discuss each office in detail but to bring out the importance of two that dovetail together. Notice after each office, a semicolon is used. But after the pastor, there is no semicolon before the teacher. That is because the pastor-teacher is one office. There is a separate office of teacher listed in 1 Corinthians 12:28 apart from the pastor. You can be a teacher without being a pastor, but you cannot be a pastor without being a teacher. Pastor is the title. Teacher is the function. If a man is called to be a pastor,

he should expect, by faith, also to operate in
the ministry gift of the teacher. The Greek
literally says "pastor-teacher." Kenneth
Wuest translates this as *"pastors who are also
teachers."*[3] These five offices are the "pulpit"
gifts. They are in contrast to the body offices
found in Romans 12:3–8.

Verse 12

*For the perfecting of the saints, for the
work of the ministry, for the edifying of
the body of Christ.*

The original Greek has no commas or
punctuation marks and all of the letters were
capitals. This verse, as it stands in the King
James, sounds like the ministry offices are to
perfect the saints, do the work of the ministry,
and edify the body of Christ. This is because of
the placing of the commas between each
phrase. If you remove the first comma, the
sentence will make more sense. The ministry
gifts are *"for the perfecting of the saints for the
work of the ministry."* The ministry gifts are
not to do the work of the ministry. They are to

---

[3] Kenneth S. Wuest, *The New Testament: An Expanded Translation* (Grand Rapids: Wm. B. Eerdmans, 1961), p. ?.

perfect the saints so that they can go do the work of the ministry. The name of the game is discipleship. Jesus told us to go into all nations and make disciples of them (Matthew 28:19-20). Ministers are not to do the work but are to teach the people to do the work. The minister should not have to come to your house and witness to your neighbor. He should instruct you in the Word so you can witness to your neighbor. The ministry offices are not doormats for you to walk over and use for your own whims. They are called by God to stand in their appropriate offices and instruct you in the ways of ambassadorship for the kingdom of God.

The ministry gifts are set in the body of Christ. Yes, God can and will give you personal revelations but not like those He will give you through a ministry gift. He has called and anointed that person to that office. Your own personal revelations during times of personal study will increase as your life comes into order and you submit to a pastor. Also, when you recognize the God-given authority in other nationally-known ministers, your own prayer and study life will be more effective. God has set the ministry gifts in the church for my edifying and perfecting so that, as I grow, I can win others and do the work of the ministry.

Verse 13

*Till we all come in the unity of the faith,
and of the knowledge of the Son of God,
unto a perfect man, unto the measure of
the stature of the fullness of Christ.*

The ministry offices will be needed until
we all come *"unto the measure of the stature of
the fullness of Christ."* This will never occur in
its fullness on the earth but at the judgment
seat of Christ. (See 1 Corinthians 3:13–15;
Ephesians 5:27; Philippians 3:20–21.) Until
then, new babies will be born into the family
of God, and there will be carnal Christians.

The body of Christ as a whole is being
perfected and each day is entering into more
of a maturity than ever before. The goal each
one of us should be shooting for in this earth
is the *"unity of the faith."* God sets high standards throughout the Word. He wants us to be
holy as He is holy and not to sin in this life.
God would like us to accept His standards and
realize that through the power of the Holy
Spirit and His Word, we can attain that which
seems impossible in the natural. It is far better to set a high standard and miss it than to
set a low one and achieve it. The mark Paul
set before himself was *"the high calling in
Christ Jesus"* (Philippians 3:14). He kept

choosing to forget the mistakes and failures of the past and to set his sights on this one goal which was the prize he continually was aiming for. (See Philippians 3:13–14.)

Time to Grow Up

Verse 14

That we henceforth be no more children, tossed to and fro, and carried about with every wind of doctrine, by the sleight of men, and cunning craftiness, whereby they lie in wait to deceive.

The Greek word for *"children"* here is *nopios.* It means "one who cannot speak." This is a very young believer who is incapable of communicating or giving out the gospel. He is likened to a ship on the ocean without a rudder or a sail. Without a rudder, a ship will be tossed to and fro by the waves. The waves are a picture of the circumstances of life. Without stability in life you are at the mercy of circumstances. This is a sure way to have an up-and-down Christian life. The Word produces stability in life so that despite the circumstances, you can maintain your course. *"And wisdom and knowledge shall be the stability of thy times, and strength of salvation"* (Isaiah

33:6). Because this ship has no means of navigation, it can also be blown about by *"every wind of doctrine."*

Baby believers are the most likely to fall for false doctrine because they tend to be gullible and, like most babies, put everything they find into their mouths. It is important for us not only to lead a person to the Lord but also to see to it that he becomes faithful in attending a church where he can be fed solid food to grow into maturity.

All this deceit comes through the *"sleight of men, and cunning craftiness."* The Greek word for *"sleight of men"* is *kubeia*. For the longest time, this word and its meaning were unknown. This is the only place in the New Testament where the word appears. The translators must have been led by the Holy Spirit because they hit very close to its meaning. This word is where we eventually got our word "cube." It was the ancient word for "dice." They had crap games in the ancient world, and many crafty people would cheat. The analogy is this: When a baby Christian refuses to submit to the authority of a pastor or other minister, he may think he is mature, but he is really stupid and immature. He is in a crap game with the devil, and the dice are loaded against him. He cannot win. Those who control the game are cheating.

Many people today want to float from church to church and never become settled. This is unscriptural and unhealthy. They often believe they are more mature than the pastors, so they think they have a right to float anywhere they want. By floating, they are admitting that they are babies. These people will be at the mercy of the circumstances of life and the false doctrines of men. When these people get into trouble, that is when they complain about the local churches not standing beside them. It is not up to a church to join you but up to you to join a church. Commitment begins with individuals.

Verse 15

But speaking the truth in love, may grow up into him in all things, which is the head. even Christ.

The baby, who could not speak, should grow up to learn *"to speak the truth in love."* Speaking the truth is speaking the Word. Speaking the Word of God is one of the greatest keys in the Christian life to answered prayers, effective confessions, and mastering the thoughts. When we become full of the Word of God, it comes out of us in two ways, words and deeds. (See Colossians 3:16–17.)

Speaking the Word is important, and doing it in love is of greater importance. Many people speak the Word of God to tear other believers apart and to set them straight. The spoken Word is a sword (Ephesians 6:17), not to be used on other believers but against Satan and his devices. When we use the Word on other believers, it should be to help remove the problem and preserve and care for the person.

All of this is part of the growing up process God has for us to move from babyhood—spiritual immaturity—to the fullness of the stature of Christ. Jesus is our example and our goal for maturity. We are to *"grow up in all things* [areas] *into him* [Christ]" who is *"the head of the church"* (Ephesians 5:23).

Verse 16

From whom [Christ] *the whole body fitly joined together and compacted by that which every joint supplieth, according to the effectual working in the measure of every part, maketh increase of the body unto the edifying of itself in love.*

Verse 15 told us that speaking the truth in love would cause us to grow up, to mature. Verse 16 tells us that edification (building up) of the body of Christ also is done in love. Love becomes a key issue in the individual and corporate growth in the body of Christ. Faith will not work without love whether it is in an individual person or an entire body of believers. Faith is the culmination of all of the input of the Word into a person's life. All the promises and Scriptures found in the Bible will do you no good if you do not operate in love toward other members of the Lord's body.

Verse 16 tells us that the whole body (natural and spiritual) is *"joined together and compacted* [knit together] *by that which every joint supplies."* What are the joints? The joints are a type of the ministry offices found in verse 11. They supply to the different parts of the body what is needed. The ministry gifts see to it that the different members are fitly joined and knit together. The members of the body of Christ are like bones in the natural body. Bones are shaped differently and, logically, should not be joined. The ends of all the different bones look as if they should not be joined to the bones next to them. What really joins bones together are *"joints and bands* [ligaments and tendons]*"* (Colossians 2:19).

This is a reference to love which has been brought out in both these verses, 15 and 16. What links me to you in the body of Christ is love. We may come from various backgrounds and levels of society and be different colors, but love joins us together into one supernatural body. When one member of the body suffers, we all suffer together with it. When one member rejoices, we all rejoice. We are inseparably joined to each other. If someone needs help, don't turn from him. We minister to him God's Word in love, give him a foundation from God's promises to stand on, and speak the truth in love so that we all may grow up together in all areas into Christ, the Head.

"Every joint supplies." Everything comes from the head down. Your mental commands come from the head to your body. They come through the nervous system, telling the body what functions to perform. The joints (offices) supply information from the Head to each part so that the body can *"increase"* itself.

This is all done through the *"effectual working in the measure of every part."* The *"effectual working"* is the measure of faith being acted on by each member of the body. It is important for each member to do his or her part in cooperation with those in ministry positions so that each person can fulfill the ministry God has for him. As each part ministers out of its measure, the body edifies itself toward the fullness of the stature of Christ.

8

Walking in the Light

Ephesians 4:17–32

Beginning in verse 17 of chapter 4, we move fully into temporal truth. This truth will run throughout the remainder of Ephesians. This first section will deal with using the Word and the power of the Spirit in you to put away sin. Walking in the light is the only way we have power to put away sin and walk in the righteousness that God has given to us through the new birth.

Verse 17

This I say therefore, and testify in the Lord, that ye henceforth walk not as other Gentiles walk, in the vanity of their mind.

We were told first how to walk in verse 1, and now we are told in verse 17 how not to walk. We are to stop walking *"as other Gentiles* [unbelievers] *walk."* He is starting to explain something that has confused Christians for a long time. Christians can look and act just like sinners. When Christians become carnal, they no longer are controlled by the Spirit of God, and they act just like the world. There should be a distinct separation between the outward life of a Christian and that of a sinner. Sin is sin, and God hates it. Verse 17 is a command against carnality for Christians.

Paul is the apostle to the Gentiles. The Ephesians are Gentiles. Paul is not talking about walking according to the law of Moses because the Gentiles were never given the law. He is showing a distinction between the Gentile Christian and the Gentile unbeliever. We are Gentiles also and well acquainted with sin. We live in a world full of sin. Our earth is perverted by the devil and the world's system. But as Christians, we should show a distinction and a separation in our outward lives because of the knowledge of the Word inside of us.

The Word never implies that from the moment of salvation you instantly make an outward change. There is a process of growing to go through in order to come to the place of laying aside every sin. Some people think that

when you are saved, the next day you should
be evidencing a holy and righteous life. That
just doesn't happen. When you are born again,
the seed is planted inside. The seed will grow
as you study the Word and pray. As it grows,
the new life will be manifested in the outward
life. Walk each day in the knowledge you have,
and the Lord will forgive the sins you commit
in ignorance. When you do commit a sin that
you know about, ask the Lord to forgive you.
He promises that He will. (See 1 John 1:7, 9.)

The Lord has commanded you to learn
when you are born again:

> [28] *Come unto me, all ye that labor and*
> *are heavy laden* [sinners], *and I will*
> *give you rest* [new birth].
> [29] *Take my yoke upon you, and learn of*
> *me.*   (Matthew 11:28–29)

Knowledge brings growth. As you grow,
there will be a new area each day that you will
have strength to lay aside. Like a child growing up, you will come to the place where you
no longer stumble and fall. You can *"walk circumspectly"* (Ephesians 5:15). The number of
unknown sins decreases each day as you gain
knowledge of His will.

When the Word is in you in abundance,
you have no excuse for sinning. Your life is to

be an example to the world. This verse tells us
that believers can act like the world. It should
not be, but it is. Believers have been given the
Holy Spirit and the power of God to overcome
all temptations and cannot blame anyone but
themselves when they become carnal.

The church has not known what to do
with carnal Christians for years, yet the pews
are filled with them. Nearly all churches are
naive when it comes to a Christian getting out
of line. They think this is impossible and come
up with one of two answers—either he has
lost his salvation, or he was never born again
in the first place. Both of these conclusions
are usually wrong. The person is born again,
but he is carnal and out of fellowship with
God. He has not lost his relationship with the
Lord, but he has lost his fellowship. Relationship and fellowship are not the same thing.

When my son was born, he had a relationship with me because he was born of my seed.
As he grows up and disobeys me, the relationship is still there, but the fellowship has been
broken. He needs to repent so that the lines of
communication can be opened again. *"If I re-
gard iniquity in my heart, the Lord will not
hear me"* (Psalm 66:18). First John 1:9 says,
*"If we confess our sins, He is faithful and just
to forgive us our sins, and to cleanse us from
all unrighteousness."* This verse was written

by John. We know he was a Christian. He said, *"If we."* This meant that John had missed it and sinned as well. This verse was not written to sinners but to Christians, believers in the Lord Jesus Christ.

The most miserable people on the face of the earth today are not sinners but believers who are out of fellowship with Christ. They are miserable, and they spread their misery. The worst stinkers in the Bible were not sinners but believers who became carnal and refused to get back into fellowship with the Lord. This always brings discipline from the Lord (Hebrews 12:6) which is intended for our good to bring us back into line with Him and to reestablish our fellowship.

You have not really been swindled until you have been gypped by a fellow Christian. You have not really been cheated until a brother in Christ cheats you. There are many times I would rather be around a happy-go-lucky sinner than a miserable, carnal Christian.

Verse 18

Having the understanding darkened, being alienated from the life of God through the ignorance that is in them, because of the blindness of their heart.

Verses 18 and 19 describe what the unbeliever is like. Once you find out what his condition is, you should realize that you have no business acting like someone who does not have eternal life or citizenship in heaven.

The Greek word for *"understanding"* is *dianoia* meaning "the faculty of understanding." *Dia* means "through" and *noia* means "mind." It literally means "through the mind," or "the faculty of understanding." Unbelievers have their faculties (means of) understanding darkened through the nature of sin that is in them. It is possible for children of light to walk like children of darkness who are blinded. God told us, *"Come out from among them* [sinners] *and be ye separate* [holy in actions]" (2 Corinthians 6:17).

I used to have a business and employed both believers and unbelievers. Was I in for a shock! Christians stole from me, were late to work, and were undependable. I employed unbelievers who behaved better and had much better attitudes. They were happy-go-lucky, going to hell, and didn't care. They were going to have a good time until they got there. The miserable ones were the Christians who were out of fellowship. They were irritable because their spirits convicted them over everything they did. The unbelievers' spirits weren't convicting them because they were not re-created.

Paul says in verse 18 that unbelievers are *"alienated* [separated] *from the life of God."* They are separated because they have not accepted the Author of life. Not to accept Jesus is called in this verse *"ignorance."* It could not be stated any better. Sinners are ignorant to keep rejecting the only answer to their problems. All of this happens because of the *"blindness of their hearts."*

Born Alive unto God

I have had to change my thinking on some areas of God's Word. One of these areas was on the subject of whether children are born into this earth spiritually alive or spiritually dead. I used to believe and teach that they are born spiritually dead. One day while at lunch with Kenneth Hagin, I questioned him about this subject. He asked me, "Who gives the spirit?"

"God does," I answered.

"Can God give a dead spirit?"

I started thinking about that. God can't give a dead spirit. People produce the body, the physical part of man, but God is the One who gives the spirit, the intangible part of man. God cannot give a dead spirit. He can only give life. He is not the author of death. The more I thought about it, the more I saw

that children could be born alive in spirit. But
I needed to see this through the Word of God.

Here is what I saw in the Word. First of
all, speaking of John the Baptist, it is stated,
*"There was a man sent from God, whose name
was John. The same came for a witness, to
bear witness of the Light, that all men through
him might believe. He was not that Light, but
was sent to bear witness to that Light. That
was the true Light, which lighteth every man
that cometh into the world"* (John 1:6–9). Who
is the Light? Jesus is the Light. Notice when
men are lit: every man is lit when he comes
into the world. I believe you can see why little
children go to heaven when they die. When
David and Bathsheba's infant son died so
quickly, David said, *"I shall go to him, but he
shall not return to me"* (2 Samuel 12:23).

That opened up another question, When
does darkness come in? Our answer is in Romans. Chapter 1 of Romans deals with the
Gentiles, while Chapter 2 deals with the Jews.
Chapter 3 shows that there is no difference
because *"All have sinned and come short of
the glory of God"* (v. 23).

> [18] *For the wrath of God is revealed from
> heaven against all ungodliness and un-
> righteousness of men, who hold the
> truth in unrighteousness;*

¹⁹ *Because that which may be known of God is manifest in them; for God hath shewed it unto them.* (Romans 1:18-19)

Do you see that? What do they hold in unrighteousness? *"The truth!"* Every man knows the truth. God has put within the spirit of every man a knowledge that there is a God. People around the world try to substitute a wooden god, a rock god, or a four-footed creeping god for the true God in order to try to fill the vacuum. Men know there is a God.

²⁰ *For the invisible things of him from the creation of the world are clearly seen, being understood by the things that are made, even his eternal power and Godhead; so that they are without excuse.* (Romans 1:20)

God has built into the things which are seen a teaching of the things that are unseen. People can understand the invisible things of God by the visible things that He made. Whether you look at the universe and see the magnificence and greatness of God or whether you look at the smallest detail of a leaf or a bug, you realize there is precision and order in everything. **Something** has to be behind it.

It does not matter which way you approach it—through the mind, nature, science,

or logic—there had to be something in the
beginning. Every effect has a cause. You have
to come eventually to an absolute. The *"invisible things"* which are *"His eternal power
and Godhead* [even the Trinity]*"* are taught by
the things which are seen.

> [21] *Because that, when they knew* [about]
> *God, they glorified him not as God, neither
> were thankful; but became vain* [empty]
> *in their imaginations and their foolish
> heart was darkened.*   (Romans 1:21)

I want to clear up one thing here. People
talk about nations that have never heard the
gospel. There is no such thing as a nation that
has never heard. If you go back in history, you
will find that at one time or another every
country has heard the Word of God and has
had revival. Nations are not heathen because
they have never heard the gospel but because
they have heard and rejected the gospel. When
a person who knows there is a God decides
that he does not want to know about Him, he
becomes vain in his imagination and his foolish heart becomes darkened. It had to have
been illuminated in order to become darkened.

Let's look at an example of this. A child is
born in New Guinea. He is around heathen-
ism as he grows. But God looks at him as an

individual and not as a mass. As that child begins to grow, he says inside himself, "There has to be a God." As he looks at creation, he thinks, "Creation has order. There must be a power behind it." He is alive on the inside because his inward man was given by God who lights each man who comes into the world. He then comes to the age of accountability, or God-consciousness. He is sure that there is a God somewhere. Maybe all he says is, "I'd like to know about Him." God is now obligated to bring the gospel. God will move heaven, earth, and hell to get the message of Jesus to him.

This is where the call to the mission field comes in. There is a difference between a person who is truly called to the mission field and a person who just goes. We have too many people out there muddying the water. That is why you need to stay sensitive to the Holy Spirit and sensitive to His leading. If one person wants to know the gospel, God will move a government to get the good news to him.

They Kill Their Own Hearts

> [21] *Because that, when they knew* [about] *God, they glorified him not as God, neither were thankful; but became vain in their imaginations, and their foolish heart was darkened.* (Romans 1:21)

Darkness is the opposite of light. *"The true Light, which lighteth every man that cometh into the world"* (John 1:9). They were lit when they came into the world. Jesus said, *"Except ye be converted, and become as little children, ye shall not enter into the kingdom of heaven"* (Matthew 18:3). Little children are alive to God. When the age of accountability is reached, a person either glorifies Him as God or not as God. If they glorify Him not as God, they become foolish in their imaginations, their faculties of understanding become blinded because of their decision, and their foolish hearts become darkened.

Second Corinthians 4:4 says that Satan is the god of this world and has blinded people's minds. Those are his—the devil's—people. Notice it is their ignorance that is keeping them away from the life of God because of the blindness of their hearts. The word translated *"blindness"* actually means "hardness." Verse 18 should read "the hardness of their hearts."

Verse 19

Who being past feeling have given themselves over unto lasciviousness, to work all uncleanness with greediness.

Paul is still talking about the blindness of the heart of those who reject Jesus as their

Savior. *"Who being past feeling"* is exactly what is talked about in Romans, chapter 1, where God gave them over to a reprobate mind. *"Lasciviousness"* is sexual immorality and *"uncleanness"* is sexual impurity in the thought life. They work lasciviousness and uncleanness with *"greediness."* Sexual impurity consumes their *"desires."* Everything in them wants to work uncleanness. They give themselves over to sexual lasciviousness. (See Romans 1:24–27.) Their unclean thoughts drive them to greediness. They never can seem to fill or satisfy their appetite for the works of darkness.

Be Renewed in Mind

Verse 20

But ye have not so learned Christ.

The purpose of taking in the Word of God is to imitate God (Ephesians 5:1), not the sinner. The believer has a power the unbeliever does not have. Now that we are born again, we need to look and act like God in this earth. This can only be done as we take in the *"mind of Christ,"* the Word of God. As we think like Him, we act like Him. *"Wisdom and knowledge shall be the stability of thy times"* (Isaiah 33:6).

Verse 21

If so be that ye have heard [understood]
*him, and have been taught by him, as
the truth is in Jesus.*

Verse 20 uses the name *"Christ,"* and
verse 21 uses the name *"Jesus."* We have the
mind of Christ, and we learn to live like Jesus.
This again is an example of positional truth
and temporal truth. We are never told to have
the mind of Jesus. We are told that we have
"the mind of Christ." If we had the mind of
Jesus, we would know all the routes in Jerusalem and Palestine, the disciples, and all the
events surrounding Jesus' life in the Middle
East. Since we have the mind of Christ, we
know who we are in Him and our rights and
privileges in God's kingdom. We know all the
things in chapters 1 through 3 which, again,
are the mind of Christ. Therefore, we can actually live out our lives as Jesus would on the
earth.

When we look at the life of Jesus, we
think all the things He did were impossible,
but they aren't if you have the mind of Christ.
If you believe the Word, all things are possible. You can perform miracles and do the
same works in this earth that Jesus did. Every
day will be supernatural. Jesus said, *"He that*

believeth on me, the works that I do shall he do also; and greater works than these shall he do" (John 14:12). *"In my name shall they cast out devils...they shall lay hands on the sick, and they shall recover"* (Mark 16:17–18). Jesus told us to live above this world. If we are going to live like Jesus, we have to have the mind of Christ.

Verses 22–23

²² *That ye put off concerning the former conversation* [manner of life] *the old man, which is corrupt according to the deceitful lusts;*
²³ *And be renewed in the spirit* [attitude] *of your mind.*

"Put off" means to "remove as clothing." (See Colossians 3:8–10.) Notice that God will not do this for you. You are to do it yourself. God always gives you the information with which to gain strength, but you are to take God's gifts and use them yourself. When it comes to imitating God in this earth and walking as Jesus would, you do it. Then, to keep strong and not fall back into the sin, *"be renewed in the spirit of your mind."*

The word *"renewed"* here is the same word found in Romans 12:1–2:

> ¹ *I beseech ye therefore, brethren, by the*
> *mercies of God, that ye present your*
> *bodies a living sacrifice, holy, accept-*
> *able unto God, which is your reasonable*
> *service.*
> ² *And be not conformed to this world:*
> *but be ye transformed by the renewing*
> *of your mind.*

Don't be conformed to this world (the old
man) but be transformed by the renewing of
your mind (putting on the new man). It says
to be transformed in the attitude of your
mind. The Word of God changes the attitude
of a person to seek as greedily after God as he
once sought after uncleanness.

Our major purpose in the Christian life is
growing up. The battle is in your mind. You
have the new man on the inside of you war-
ring against the old man on the outside. The
old man, of course, refers to the desire of the
body, the nature of the flesh. (See Romans 6:6,
12–13; 7:18.) The mind is the battleground
between the two (Romans 7:22–25). The Word
renews the mind, and the desires then come
into line to live a godly life in this world. The
new man says, *"Blessed are they that have not*
seen, and yet have believed" (John 20:29).
There comes a time when you step out in faith
and tell your senses, "Shut up, I'm going to

believe God's Word." After doing it several
times, your mind knows that it works! The new
(inward) man is strengthened; the old (outward)
man is put off. We do it, not God. We only use
what He has provided—His eternal Word.

Verses 24–25

²⁴ *And that ye put on the new man*
[inward man], *which* [designed] *after
God is created in righteousness and
true holiness.*
²⁵ *Wherefore* [because you put on the
new man] *putting away lying, speak
every man truth with his neighbor: for
we are members one of another.*

When you become renewed in the attitude
of your mind, you should discover the ability
to put "*away lying* [and] *speak every man
truth with his neighbor.*" The Word gives you
the power to do it. This is written to believers.
Believers do lie sometimes. Hebrews 12:1
says: "*Let us lay aside every weight, and the
sin which doth so easily beset us.*" The inward
man is strong. Use him to put away sin.

Verse 26

*Be ye angry, and sin not: let not the sun
go down upon your wrath.*

How can you be angry and not sin? Isn't
anger a sin? Yes, when it is directed toward
people or God. Anger is not wrong when it is
directed toward sin or Satan. Jesus was furi-
ous with what the religious leaders were doing. He loved the religious people, but He
hated religion. He loved sinners, but He hated
sin. He loved the demon-possessed, but He
hated demons. Jesus loved the world so much
that He went to the cross and died for the
very people who spit on Him and betrayed
Him. You can be angry at what a person does
and not sin. Hate sin, but love people.

In Matthew 7:1–5, Jesus talked about removing a splinter from your brother's eye.
"Splinters" are sins. We are to love our
brother but hate the splinter and help to get
rid of it without doing the brother harm. That
is how to be angry and sin not. *"Judge not,
that ye be not judged. For...with what measure
ye mete, it shall be measured to you again"*
(Matthew 7:1–2). It is all right to judge sin,
but don't judge the person. If you are angry
with a person, you better watch out. It will be
measured back to you many times over (Luke
6:37–38). Judging people is stepping over into
God's territory. He will judge all people in the
end, and He doesn't need your help in the
meantime. If you want to stir the wrath of
God, just try judging people. He has given us

the right to judge sin while we are here but not people. *"But he that is spiritual judgeth all things* [not people]*"* (1 Corinthians 2:15).

"Let not the sun go down on your wrath." There may be times when we move from anger to wrath. It is often easy when we become angry at sin to pass judgment on the person involved. The moment this happens, ask the Lord to forgive you and get rid of the wrath. Stay in an attitude of love toward your brother, but keep your anger toward the devil.

Galatians 6:1 says:

Brethren, if a man be overtaken in a fault [sin], *ye which are spiritual, restore such a one in the spirit of meekness* [staying teachable]; *considering* [constantly examining] *thyself, lest thou also be tempted.*

It is easy when you are helping someone else out of their problems to become tempted to judge them. Stay in a spirit of meekness. Remember how stupid you have been? Remember the times when you sinned yourself? Wasn't the Lord good to you? Did He treat you as you are treating the person you are helping? Our object is to restore people, not to judge them.

Verse 27

Neither give place to the devil.

The Greek word for *"place"* here is *topos* and means "ground." We get our English word "topography" from this word. Don't give any ground to the devil. Once you have taken a piece of property from Satan and conquered it for the kingdom of God, don't give it up. Be angry at the devil, but keep yourself from wrath. This will insure that your victories over Satan are not just temporary and that you will not lose ground taken from him in prior battles.

Verse 28

Let him that stole steal no more: but rather let him labor, working with his hands the thing that is good, that he may have to give to him that needeth.

When you are not working at a job, providing income for yourself and family, the Word says you are stealing. Second Thessalonians 3:10–12 tells us that people who do not work should not eat. They are also said to be disorderly, busybodies, and end up eating food which belongs to others. God's plan of financial prosperity begins with a job. Before Adam was given a wife in the garden, he was given a job. He learned the importance of providing before his wife and family were given to him.

This verse also tells us the chief purpose of a Christian's money in the earth. God blesses us so we can give. A working, giving believer will end up in God's plan of prosperity. His bread will come from the work of his own hands and the grace of God. At the end of his life, he can say with David, *"Yet have I not seen the righteous forsaken, nor his seed begging bread"* (Psalm 37:25).

Verse 29

> *Let no corrupt communication proceed out of your mouth, but that which is good to the use of edifying, that it may minister grace unto the hearers.*

Corrupt communication tears down. Grace builds up and edifies. Corrupt communication is anything that does not encourage or uplift the hearer. Stop and think before the words come out of your mouth: Is what you are about to say edifying? We have had three chapters telling us who we are in Christ. The Lord has spent all this time giving us words of edification. How the Lord ministers to us is how we should minister to others. Now, what is going to come out of your mouth? Let it be grace. *"Let your speech be alway with grace, seasoned with salt* [the Word], *that ye may know how ye ought to answer every man"* (Colossians 4:6).

Verse 30

And grieve not the holy Spirit of God, whereby ye are sealed unto the day of redemption.

What is it that can grieve the Holy Spirit? The words you speak. Corrupt communication is sin which grieves the Spirit. When a person is out of fellowship with the Lord, he can react in one of two ways: he can sin, or he can attempt to live the Christian life in the flesh. Both displease the Lord. Many times when a person is carnal, he tries to impress God with his good intentions and deeds. At this point, God is not impressed with anything except repentance (1 John 1:9). Fleshly energy is a stench in God's nostrils. Sin grieves the Holy Spirit, and energy of the flesh quenches the Holy Spirit. (See 1 Thessalonians 5:19–22.)

This passage tells us one of the prime ways to sin and grieve the Holy Spirit is to speak words of judgment. Don't grieve the Spirit with corrupt communication, but minister words of grace that please Him.

Verse 31

Let all bitterness, and wrath, and anger, and clamor, and evil speaking, be put away from you, with all malice.

Notice again that this verse is speaking to believers. Christians can be bitter, can be full of wrath and anger, and can speak evil of others. This verse is a mixture of inner and outward sins. We have sins of the thoughts and sins of actions. *"Bitterness"* is inner hatred for others. Even though people around you may not know that you are bitter, God knows. He looks at the heart whereas people look at the outward appearance (1 Samuel 16:7).

"Wrath" is the display of bitterness. It is an outward, visible sin. When bitterness finally comes to a head, it displays itself in the form of wrath. I like to define wrath as emotional outbursts.

"Anger" is an inward sin but it differs from bitterness. If you are bitter at someone, it is obvious that you do not like them. Anger is something you can have even toward a friend. Anger, if not forsaken, will eventually lead to bitterness and wrath. Anger is an inward hostility toward someone.

"Clamor" is another overt sin, the outward display of anger. It is actually physical

fighting with or hitting someone else. I know some of you are thinking right now that Christians don't get into fist fights. Well, you must have led a sheltered life. You are in for some great shocks in the Christian life. *"Clamor"* also is called "striking" in 1 Timothy 3:3 and "brawling" in Titus 3:2.

"Evil speaking" is another outward sin from which we are to refrain. Many times an evil thought will come to your mind, but don't let the words come out of your mouth. Ask the Lord to forgive you for the thought before it festers into an evil word that would slander or vilify others.

"Malice" is the final word that we need to explain in this verse. This is an inward sin of the thoughts. It actually means "malicious or evil intentions." This sin can be covered by a thin coating of sincerity. Have you ever been told some juicy gossip by someone who began by saying, "I'm only telling you this about Brother ——— so you can pray for him"? Why don't they pray for him themselves and keep their mouths shut? This kind of person has *"malice"* or evil intentions. This verse is telling us that it is just as important for us to clean up our intentions and mental sins as it is to forsake the outward, visible sins.

Verse 31 told us what we are not to do. Verse 32 is going to tell us what we are to do.

Verse 32

And be ye kind one to another, tender-hearted, forgiving one another, even as God for Christ's sake hath forgiven you.

"Tenderhearted" is an interesting word in the Greek, *eusplagnos. Eu* means "good," and *splagnos* means "bowels" or "guts." "Good guts" may not sound too wonderful today, but it meant a lot in the day the Bible was written. This is more than just pitying people. It is having a godly compassion that comes from deep within you, from your "guts." This also is referred to in the Word as *"bowels of compassion"* (1 John 34:17). In the Old Testament, it was said of Joseph who was in a deep emotional state that *"his bowels did yearn"* (Genesis 43:30). Joseph did not have a physical problem; instead, he had an intense desire or compassion that came from deep within him.

We are to have such a deep compassion for people that forgiveness is never a question. We desire to forgive them as Jesus, out of His deep compassion, forgave us. We are told in this verse how to forgive people—as God forgives us (Matthew 6:12–15). How long does it take God to forgive us? He forgives us instantly. We are to do the same. This is how compassion treats those who wrong us.

Do you remember the story about the footwashing in John 13:4–17? Jesus was talking to His disciples as He washed their feet. Naturally, Peter spoke up and said, *"Lord, dost thou wash* [only] *my feet?...Lord, not my feet only, but also my hands and my head"* (vv. 6, 9). In other words, Peter was saying, "Give me a bath. Save me again."

The Lord replied to Peter:

> [10] *No, he that is washed needs not to wash but his feet, for he that is washed is clean every wit....*
> [14] *If I then, your Lord and Master, have washed your feet; ye also ought to wash one another's feet.*
> [15] *For I have given you an example, that ye should do as I have done to you.*
>
> (John 13:10, 14–15)

First John 1:9 is our footwashing from the Lord. When we ask Him to forgive us for our sins, He is always *"faithful and just to forgive us our sins, and to cleanse us from all unrighteousness."* If He is faithful and just to wash our feet, we should be just as faithful to wash the feet of those who wrong us. If Jesus can do it, then we can do it also. (See Matthew 18:21–35.)

9

Follow after God

Ephesians 5:1–21

Chapter 4 told us what to turn away from. Now chapter 5 begins by telling us what to follow after. We are to follow after God the Father and the Lord Jesus Christ and not to follow after the sinner and his ways (vv. 3–13).

Verse 1

Be [become] *ye therefore followers* [imitators] *of God, as dear children.*

Mimites is the Greek word for *"followers."* This is where we get our English word "mimic." It means to mimic or to imitate God. We were told in the previous verse to imitate

God in forgiveness. If He forgives you, then act like Him and forgive others. Imitating God is a sure key to success in the Christian life. Just like natural children imitate their parents, we as spiritual children of our heavenly Father should imitate Him.

We know God is love (1 John 4:8), peace (1 Thessalonians 5:23), and hope (Romans 15:13). He has infinite patience and mercy. What He has and is belongs to us as His children. As the Lord treats us, we should treat others. Our objective after we are born again is to act like God would.

Verse 2

And walk in love, as Christ also hath loved us, and hath given himself for us an offering and a sacrifice to God for a sweet-smelling savor.

Not only are we to imitate our Father but our older brother Jesus. Children often use older siblings as an example. Jesus is our perfect example of love. If we love others as Jesus loves us, then our lives can be a *"sweet-smelling savor"* to our Father.

"Sweet-smelling savor" is a reference to the Old Testament sacrifices. When the priests were finished offering sacrifices, the Bible says

God was satisfied. When everything was performed according to the pattern of the Word, then God was satisfied with the work that had been done. This obedience to His Word is a sweet smell to Him.

When Jesus went to the cross, died for the sins of the world, and was resurrected on the third day, God was satisfied. When Jesus offered Himself up as the final sacrifice, He was a *"sweet-smelling savor"* before God. God was satisfied with the work of Jesus.

Many times we sing the song, "I Am Satisfied." That song is good but misses the most important part of the Scriptures which is not that I am satisfied but that God is satisfied. Satisfied first with the work of Jesus and, next of all, with me. Because I have accepted the work of His Son Jesus, God is satisfied with me. When Jesus sat down on the right hand of the Father, God must have said, "I am satisfied." When I accepted Jesus, He said the same thing about me. It is my prayer that God be satisfied with me each and every day. This can be done as I walk in the love of Jesus.

"He is the propitiation for our sins: and not for ours only, but also for the sins of the whole world" (1 John 2:2). The Greek word for *"propitiation"* means "satisfaction." God was satisfied with the work of Jesus on the cross. That whole concept is meant here in this verse when

it says that Jesus gave *"Himself for us* [as] *an offering and a sacrifice to God for a sweet-smelling savor."*

If Jesus offered Himself up as a sacrifice before the Father, and God was satisfied, then we also need to dedicate ourselves before God to serve the needs of others. As we do this, God will be satisfied with us. Romans 12:1 says, *"I beseech you therefore, brethren, by the mercies of God, that ye present your bodies a living sacrifice, holy, acceptable unto God, which is your reasonable service."* *"Acceptable"* means that God is satisfied as we present our bodies to His work. Is God satisfied with your life?

Even before the cross, Jesus daily dedicated Himself to the will of God. We also need to dedicate ourselves day by day. "Father, I am dedicating myself to You today. My flesh, the old man, is on the altar. I choose to put on the new man and walk by Your Word and the guidance of the Holy Spirit. I desire to be acceptable, a satisfaction to You."

Put Away Sin

Verse 3

But fornication, and all uncleanness, or covetousness, let it not be once named among you, as becometh saints.

Verse 3 through verse 13 is a passage telling us who not to imitate—the unbeliever. Paul has already taught this thought before, but here he emphasizes it again by telling of the different sins into which carnal believers might fall. Verse 3 begins by telling us some of the things we are to *"put off."*

These are the deeds of the "old man." The first sin mentioned is *"fornication."* The Greek word is *phorneia.* In the days of the New Testament, this was a dirty word. It refers to any sex act outside the proper boundaries of marriage. Sex was designed by God to be holy to the Lord and a blessing and pleasure to the married couple. The Word says to flee fornication and all *"uncleanness,"* which refers to impurity or anything that surrounds improper sexual activity. Improper sex always leads to more impurity. In this context, *"covetousness"* still refers to sex. This is the greediness in always desiring to have more sex. Immorality can be a never-ending circle of deeper involvement. It eventually will destroy the body and the life.

"Let it not be named [mentioned] *among you."* This does not mean that you cannot talk of evil sexual practices but that Christians should not be doing such things so they would come to be mentioned. We all need to discuss sins of the world at times and how we can preach effectively to our people. The heartache

of sin is that many times it is being committed by those who are redeemed. This is not becoming or proper for the saints of God.

Verse 4

Neither filthiness, nor foolish talking, nor jesting, which are not convenient: but rather giving of thanks.

"*Filthiness*" here is obscenity. Believe it or not, Christians speak obscenities. Perhaps you have been around a believer at one time or another when something did not go right, and words came from his mouth which shocked you. Perhaps that person has been you. Maybe things have come from your mouth which have surprised you. The flesh will rise up on you when you are weak, and your mouth may surprise you. Ask the Lord to forgive you. "*Filthiness*" is not necessarily cursing the Lord, but it also involves using sexually obscene words or base language that the world uses.

"*Foolish talking*" is another type of language Christians should not be using. It may not be obscene or cursing but the type of silly talk which is not uplifting to the Lord. It may include the expression of desires to do things Christians should not do or to go places Christians should not go. "*Foolish talking*" is really the talk of the fool, or unbeliever. *"The fool has said in his heart, There is no God"* (Psalm 14:1). Racial remarks and sexual innuendoes are not what Christians should be talking about when they come together.

"Jesting" is sexual statements to gain attention. Many people feel they need to draw attention to themselves, so they use some rude sexual remark to watch people's shocked expressions. That is not what God wants from His children. Again, you may not think Christians do such things. In that case, you are in for a surprise. These verses are directed to believers to separate themselves from the world and the actions of the ungodly.

"Which are not convenient" means not up to God's standard. God has a standard of holiness which we are to maintain. The things mentioned in this verse are far below God's standard of living. The things which come from our mouths should cause praise to be given to God.

This verse is not saying that a Christian should be a "stick-in-the-mud." God does not intend that every word from our mouths be "Praise God" or "Hallelujah." Nothing is more obnoxious than a Christian who tries to be "super-spiritual." This type of person cannot go to a party or other social event without making everyone else feel inferior because they are not always talking about some spiritual revelation or word from God. Christians should be the most relaxed people at any get-together and should enjoy talking on a variety of subjects—from football and world events to children and fashions—while still being uplifting to the Lord.

Christians should be able to pour a soft drink *"as to the Lord"* (Colossians 3:23) as aptly as they would if they were preaching a sermon or leading a worship service. Everything has its place. It seems that if Christians have a party, someone inevitably tries to turn it into a prayer meeting or a Bible study. These things are both important, but there is a time for everything (Ecclesiastes 3:1, 17).

Jesus went to parties and enjoyed Himself. He was the life of the party, while the legalistic Pharisees picketed outside. Later, they condemned Jesus and His disciples for not fasting as they did. There always are a few wet blankets around who are super-spiritual and try to form others in their mold. One of the qualities of an elder in 1 Timothy 3:2 is being *"given to hospitality."* Some people are gifted at throwing parties and having get-togethers. In the early church, believers met for the *"breaking of bread"* (Acts 2:46). This is a time strictly for fellowship. God not only made us spiritual creatures, but He also made us social beings.

Christians can have much better parties than the world because we do not have to use filthy talk or jesting to have a good time. We do not have to rely on drugs or drinking to get our minds off our problems. We can come to the party with the problems of the world far from us and really have a party. Our parties are simply extensions of the celebration we have continually in our hearts.

Verse 5

For this ye know, that no whoremonger, nor unclean person, nor covetous man, who is an idolater, hath any inheritance in the kingdom of Christ and of God.

Verse 5 now tells us who not to imitate: the unbeliever who is being spoken of in this verse. The sins that the unbeliever commits can be committed by a Christian also, but God will forgive the believer and restore him to fellowship. The person discussed in this verse is an unbeliever because he is *"an idolater,"* someone who worships another god other than the one true God.

The Greek for *"whoremonger"* is *pornos*. We get our English word "pornography" from this word. A whoremonger is a pimp or a prostitute. An *"unclean person"* is in the same group but doesn't necessarily commit sexual acts. This person is filthy in his thinking. He looks at everything through the eyes of sex. He may not commit adultery physically, but he mentally undresses women at every glance. The *"covetous man"* does partake of sexual sins and is now possessed in his thinking and actions with committing adultery. His every thought is an obsession of when he can have sex again. He craves sexual immorality.

If we have the Spirit of God living in us, then why do we even consider doing these things? We are to *"flee fornication"* (1 Corinthians 6:18). We who have an *"inheritance in the kingdom of Christ and of God"* (see also Ephesians 1:11, 14) should not act like those who do not.

Verse 6

Let no man deceive you with vain [empty] words: for because of these things cometh the wrath of God upon the children [sons] of disobedience.

If our home is heaven and our objective is to store up as many rewards as possible for when we get there, why are we acting like those who are going to face the wrath of God? They will spend eternity in the lake of fire with the devil and his angels. If we are born again, headed for heaven, and desirous of spiritual rewards, then why don't we act like it? Don't be enticed with empty words of men to follow after the world. It is not befitting saints nor is it up to God's standard. Let there be a clean mark of distinction between the church and the world.

Verse 7

Be [become] *not ye therefore partakers with them.*

"*Partakers*" means participants. Don't participate with the deeds of sin or with those who live apart from God. Just as we learn from 1 Corinthians 3:3, "*For ye are yet carnal: for whereas there is among you envying, and strife, and divisions, are ye not carnal, and walk as men?*" Verse 7 also lets us know that believers can and do act like unbelievers. God does not warn of things which do not exist. "Do not become participants with sinners. Participate with God." Let God fill your speech and actions.

Verse 8

For ye [believers] *were sometimes* [formerly] *darkness, but now are ye light in the Lord: walk as children of light.*

Colossians 1:13 tells us we were one time in the kingdom of darkness, but we have been translated into the kingdom of His dear Son. This is positional truth. Now that you are a child of light, you are to walk in the light. This is temporal truth. It is possible to be a child of light and still walk in darkness.

> *⁶ If we say that we have fellowship with him, and walk in darkness, we lie, and do not the truth:*
> *⁷ But if we walk in the light, as he is in the light, we have fellowship one with another, and the blood of Jesus Christ his Son cleanseth us from all sin.*
>
> (1 John 1:6–7)

Let's look at Romans 13:11–12:

> *¹¹ And that, knowing the time, that now it is high time to awake out of sleep [carnality]: for now is our salvation [the rapture] nearer than when we believed.*
> *¹² The night is far spent, the day is at hand: let us therefore cast off the works of darkness [acting like the world], and let us put on the armor of light.*

Notice the term *"awake out of sleep."* We are going to find those same words used here in

Ephesians 5. *"The armor of light"* refers to the weapons of our warfare, which will be mentioned in Ephesians 6. Here it is called *"the armor of light."*

Many times in the Word of God, you will find a contrast such as darkness and light, death and life, or Satan and Christ that illustrates the differences between the believer and the unbeliever. We were once in the kingdom of darkness, but now we are in the kingdom of light. You were once in the kingdom of death and Satan. Now you are in the kingdom of life and Christ.

Those same examples of the believer and unbeliever are also used as examples of carnal and spiritual Christians. First John 1:7 says, *"But if we walk in the light, as he is in the light, we have fellowship one with another."* Fellowship has to do with temporal truth in the Christian life. First John, chapter 1, is not talking about our relationship with the Lord, it is talking about fellowship. Therefore, the same analogy of darkness and light is now applied to the subject of walking in or out of fellowship. We are not talking about a Christian being carnal or spiritual in fellowship or out. If you are out of fellowship, you are walking in darkness. You are not in the kingdom of darkness, but you are walking in the darkness away from the light of His presence.

That same analogy is now brought out of day and night, darkness and light.

> [13] *Let us* [believers] *walk honestly, as in the day; not in rioting and drunkenness, not in chambering and wantonness, not in strife and envying.*
> [14]*But put ye on the Lord Jesus Christ, and make not provisions for the flesh, to fulfill the lusts thereof.* (Romans 13:13–14)

Let's review. If you are out of fellowship with the Lord, you are in the flesh and are walking in darkness. If you are in fellowship with the Lord, you are in the spirit and are walking in the light. If you are out of fellowship, you are asleep. If you are in fellowship, you are awake.

Keeping that in mind, let us look again at Ephesians 5:8: "*For ye were sometimes darkness, but now are ye light in the Lord: walk as children of light.*" We suddenly shifted from positional truth, "*Ye were formerly darkness, but now are ye light,*" to temporal truth, "*Walk as children of light.*"

Verse 9

For the fruit [production] *of the Spirit* [light] *is in all goodness and righteousness and truth.*

The word *"Spirit"* could also have been translated "light." We are not talking about the fruit of the Spirit, we're talking about fruit produced by walking in the light. *"If we walk in the light as he is in the light, we have fellowship one with the other"* (1 John 1:7). When we walk in darkness—out of fellowship with the Lord— we still produce works, but they are not acceptable to the Lord. We may produce what looks like good works, but they are products of the energy of the flesh. The flesh can counterfeit divine works, but they are not up to God's standards. We are told in the Word to pray, give offerings, attend church regularly, and love other believers. This can be done in or out of fellowship with the Lord.

If these things are done outside of fellowship, we are imitating the unbeliever, which is unacceptable to the Lord. The production we have is counted by the Lord as *"wood, hay, and stubble"* (1 Corinthians 3:12). If these things are done while in fellowship with the Lord, we imitate God which is acceptable with the Lord. He counts our production as *"gold, silver, and precious stones."* When we stand before the Lord on Judgment Day, our works will be judged by fire. All of the wood, hay, and stubble will be burned. What remains will be what we accomplished for the Lord while we walked in the light. (See 1 Corinthians 3:13–15.) The production of the light *"is in all goodness and righteousness and truth."* We cannot fail, if we walk in the light God has given us.

Verse 10

Proving what is acceptable unto the Lord.

"Proving" means revealing. You are revealing what is acceptable to the Lord when you walk in the light and your production is good and righteous. The Bible says in Psalm 119:105, *"Thy word is a lamp unto my feet, and a light unto my path."* God's Word is a light unto my feet showing me where to go. It is also a lamp to reveal objects in the road that could hurt or trap. The same light that shows me where to go shows me what to avoid. So light has two functions: to instruct in truth and to reveal error. The Word reveals what is acceptable to the Lord.

Verse 11

Have no fellowship [association] *with the unfruitful* [barren] *works of darkness, but rather reprove* [expose] *them.*

Don't associate with the barren production of darkness. The world produces darkness because it has no light in them. As believers, we are not to put our lamps under a bushel. (See Matthew 5:15-16.) When this happens, the world cannot see our light, and we look no different than a child of darkness. We, like Gideon, need to smash the pots which surround our lamps and let the world and the enemy see our light. This verse is another command not to act like the world. First Corinthians 3:3 says that Christians who are carnal look and act like unbelievers. In the *Amplified Bible* they are called *"mere men."* Thank God we are not mere men, but we are supermen. A carnal believer is no longer spiritual. He also produces darkness because he is not controlled by the Holy Spirit in him. The flesh cannot produce light. You are a child of light, now walk like one.

I have had many people say to me, "The way to win unbelievers is to associate with them and do what they do." This is not true. Don't go into bars and jest and drink so you can win them. It won't work. You have dropped your standard. Have you ever noticed when you walk into a room where people know you are a Christian, all the talk stops? Have you prayed when you have been in a restaurant? Many people will look at you. You make them nervous. You expose them. Don't associate with the barren works of darkness. Instead, expose them. When there is no bushel over your light, you cannot help but put the sinner under conviction. Light exposes what darkness hides.

Jesus said, *"Ye are the light of the world"* (Matthew 5:14). He did not say try to be light. A lamp does not try to shine. It just shines. We do not need to try to be a witness and expose the works of darkness, we just do. The Holy Spirit came on you to be a witness, not to do witnessing. You are a witness. You can't hide it, if you walk in the light. Don't try to force it or cover it up. Just be what you are.

Verse 12

For it is a shame even to speak of those things which are done of them in secret.

There is a shame attached with all sin. The sins of this chapter are especially shameful: lasciviousness, uncleanness, and sexual greediness. It is a shame even to discuss them. We should not be afraid to discuss sin, but it is a shame that we have to. If there is shame in speaking of those things, think of the shame in doing them.

Verse 13

But all things that are reproved are made manifest by the light: for whatsoever doth make manifest is light.

Sinners should feel convicted when they are around you. You are a light exposing the sinful areas in their lives. The only force that exposes darkness is light. This is why it is important for your light to be strong. Light exposes problems, but it cannot do away with them. That is for the individual to deal with himself.

If your light is under a bushel, it cannot expose sin in others. It is smothered by your own sin. If you, as salt, have lost your savor, you cannot preserve the world around you because you are spoiled yourself. You are not a witness to the world, and they will run roughshod over you. Carnality covers the light and makes you appear like the sinner. First John 1:9 breaks carnality and causes the light to shine again.

Verse 14

Wherefore he saith, Awake thou that sleepest, and arise from [among] *the dead, and Christ shall give thee light.*

This is a reference to Isaiah 60:1 and is an encouragement for the carnal believer to shed his sin and start imitating God. The word *"from"* in the Greek means "out from among." Here, in essence, are the same things we found

in 1 Corinthians 3. A carnal Christian looks
and acts like a sinner.

You may be wondering, But doesn't this
verse say that he is dead? No, it does not say
he is dead. It says he is asleep among the dead.
If there were 100 dead people on the ground
and one of them was merely asleep, could we
tell which one it was by casually glancing over
them? No, we would have to look closely and
examine them for signs of life. At first glance,
the sleeping one would look and act like the
dead ones. That is what a carnal Christian is:
asleep among the dead. From all outward ap-
pearances, he looks like a mere man. Because a
carnal believer who gets caught up in the
works of the flesh looks and acts like the world,
he is "asleep among the dead."

The first thing he needs to do is, *"Awake."*
First John 1:9 says, *"If we confess our sins*
[awake], *he is faithful and just to forgive us our
sins, and to cleanse us from all unrighteousness."* This is our "wake-up call." Immediately,
we are back in fellowship with the Lord. Next,
we need to *"arise from the dead."* Not only do
we need to return to fellowship with the Lord,
we need to separate ourselves from the world.

Last of all, Christ gives us light. This is the
reward of walking in the light. Our production
is no longer darkness but that which is produced by a life free from sin and empowered by

the light of the Holy Spirit within us. There is again a clear distinction between His life and the world. This is the kind of life God wants us to maintain.

Verse 15

See then that ye walk circumspectly, not as fools, but as wise.

Now that you are back in fellowship, walk. Put your newfound spiritual life to work. How are we to walk? Circumspectly. This means with accuracy, *"not as fools* [sinners], *but as wise."* Wise people are filled with the knowledge of God's Word and use it. In other words, accuracy comes from consistency of study and prayer.

Verse 16

Redeeming the time, because the days are evil.

I love the word *"redeeming."* It means "to buy back." If I continue to follow the Word, the Lord will buy back the time that I wasted when I was out of fellowship, sleeping among the dead. What the cankerworm has eaten will be restored, and Satan loses again.

Many saints in the Word fell into sin. Abraham, Noah, Elijah, and David are just a few. They were "asleep for awhile among the dead." Yet they went on to greater heights than ever. The Lord redeemed the time. These saints are an example to us.

Hebrews 12:1 calls them our *"cloud of witnesses,"* encouraging us to *"lay aside every weight, and the sin which doth so easily beset us, and let us run with patience the race that is set before us."* As we keep our eyes on Jesus, He redeems the time.

It is important that we buy back as much time as possible because *"the days are evil."* This is a reference to the time period in which we live, the church age. During the time we are on earth, Satan is the god of this world (2 Corinthians 4:4). These evil days will be over one of these days when Satan and his angels will be cast into the bottomless pit for 1,000 years. Until that day, we are to walk as children of light in this world of darkness. We are to show the Lord in a world controlled by Satan. This is why it is important to *"arise from the dead,"* to rise up and walk accurately.

Verse 17

Wherefore be ye not unwise, but understanding what the will of the Lord is.

The word *"unwise"* means stupid or ignorant. After you buy back the time, don't become ignorant, but understand the will of the Lord. Two things are involved in knowing the will of the Lord: (1) His Word and (2) the leading of the Holy Spirit. We already have studied the importance of the Word. The importance of the Holy Spirit in our lives will be brought out in verse 18.

Verse 18

And be not drunk with wine, wherein is excess; but be filled with the Spirit.

Ephesians 5:18 has a parallel verse in Colossians 3:16:

[16] *Let the word of Christ dwell in you richly in all wisdom; teaching and admonishing one another in psalms and hymns and spiritual songs, singing with grace in your hearts to the Lord.*

The Ephesians verse tells us to be filled with the Spirit, while the verse in Colossians tells us to be filled with the Word. You can be no more filled with the Spirit than you are with the Word. That is how you can know the will of the Lord—through the Word and the Spirit.

You see, it is not enough just to have knowledge of the Word. You can become dry. It is not enough just to have the leading of the Spirit. You have no balance. We have had emotional churches that had the Spirit and the gifts but didn't want the Word. Then you have the other extreme that just teaches the Word, and they are dry. You need the two working together. The Word and the Spirit agree. When you have the Word and the leading of the Spirit, you have maturity.

Again, in verse 18, *"And be not drunk with wine, wherein is excess, but be filled with the Spirit."* In this verse, wine is a reference to natural things of the world. They are legitimate things which have to be kept in perspective, moderation, or they will rob your spiritual life. When it comes to natural things of this world, know your limits. But when it comes to your spiritual life, never find the limit. Be filled with the Spirit. Be a spiritual glutton.

Things to excess both in the natural and in the spiritual cause an effect. Food to excess causes fat. Wine to excess causes drunkenness. So if the same thing happens in the spirit realm, what is produced when you have more than enough? The result is being spiritual. You become so spiritual that you cannot contain it. It just overflows on everybody else. Even the term *"be filled with the Spirit"* here is present linear action, a continuing action meaning, *"Be* [constantly being] *filled with the Spirit."*

Verse 19

Speaking to [among] *yourselves in psalms and hymns and spiritual songs, singing and making melody in your heart to the Lord.*

This is a reference to the utterance gifts of the Spirit (word of wisdom, word of knowledge, and prophecy) operating when Spirit-filled believers come together. The infilling of the Holy Spirit (v. 18) is the doorway to the gifts (v. 19).

Colossians 3:17 says, *"And whatsoever ye do, in word or deed, do all in the name of the Lord Jesus, giving thanks to God and the Father by Him."* There are only two ways you can serve the Lord: by word or by deed. The confession of your faith is important, but so are your actions, your works (James 2:26). If you believe in your heart, it will come out of your mouth in the form of a confession, or out through your body in the form of deeds. Many times, I would rather see you do something than to hear you say something. What you do often speaks louder than what you say.

It is important to be around other believers and be admonished *"in psalms and hymns and spiritual songs,"* but what about when you leave the church? What is the world going to see? They don't understand *"psalms and hymns and spiritual songs."* They understand one thing: Put up or shut up! They want to see your faith.

Beginning here in verse 18, and throughout the rest of Ephesians, we are going to find out that spiritual Christians make the best wives, husbands, children, parents, employees, employers, and witnesses. What you are speaks as loud, if not louder, than what you say. *"Walk in wisdom toward them that are without, redeeming the time"* (Colossians 4:5). *"Them that are without"* refers to unbelievers.

Then, Paul says, *"Let your speech be alway with grace, seasoned with salt, that ye may know how ye ought to answer every man"* (Colossians 4:6). Paul tells us that the Word in us to excess will come out in wisdom toward sinners. Here in Ephesians 5:18, the Spirit in us to excess will also come out in wisdom toward sinners. The balanced life of the Word and the Spirit makes better spouses, parents, children, and workers. God has ordained that on every level of society, the gospel is to be ministered by word and deed. How you do your job can win those around you. Speaking with wisdom will open the eyes of their understanding.

Most people think that a life filled with the Word and the Spirit will cause you to float around all day "in the Spirit." Being "in the Spirit" is not a weird, unapproachable state. Spiritual people make more sense than anyone. They have the most creative ideas on the job, at home, in class, or wherever they might be. It also does not mean you will go into a pulpit ministry or to the mission field. Your job is your pulpit. The neighborhood or your department is your mission field. God will reward the faithful, Spirit-filled wife as much as the apostle to Africa. We all need the power of the Holy Spirit in our lives and the knowledge of God's Word.

Verses 20–21

²⁰ *Giving thanks always for all things unto God and the Father in the name of our Lord Jesus Christ,*
²¹ *Submitting yourselves one to another in the fear of God.*

A life of power always gives thanksgiving and praise to the givers of it all, God the Father and our Lord Jesus Christ. Praise should continually fill our mouths. Praise is submission to God. Submission to Him puts our lives in perspective to those around us. Believers should see the Lord in each other and give honor and respect to them. (See Philippians 2:2–3.) The verses to come all amplify the principle of submission and authority to each other in all areas of life.

10

The Marriage Analogy

Ephesians 5:22–33

The Word teaches about two forms of love: *agape* and *phileo*. Also the Word teaches how these types of love operate between people and God. God loves you because it is His nature to love you. He doesn't love you based on anything you do or don't do. God's love is based on His own nature which is always to give. Right now, God is aggressive toward you and abounding toward you in love.

You might say, "I've failed Him." It doesn't matter. His love isn't based on what you do. He first loved you. You had nothing that He wanted. You were lost in your trespass and sin, unfit, a child of Satan. Yet He searched out, found, and loved you. That is real love.

God's love for you is *agape* love. We talked
about God being the aggressor in this relationship. That is exactly what *agape* love is. *Agape*
love is an aggressive love. It is always abounding. *Agape* love, like grace, is always based on
the nature of the giver. God loves you because
it is His nature. God doesn't love you because
you serve Him, and God doesn't quit loving you
because you fail Him. He always loves you.

There is not one sin you can commit to
make God quit loving you because His love is
not based on what you do. He loves sinners,
and they certainly are not doing anything to
merit His love. *Agape* love is an aggressive love.
It is always abounding, always producing, and
it is never based on the receiver. It is always
based on the giver.

Agape love is glorified in *phileo* love. When
you respond, God is glorified. God is abounding
right now with *"all things that pertain unto life
and godliness."* But what is it that pleases the
Lord? Faith. Faith is responding to His love.
Faith is responding to His grace. The Lord's
love for us is seen in the husband and wife relationship. The husband represents Jesus
Christ; the wife, the church. As Jesus Christ
loves the church, He is glorified when the
church responds.

Titus 2:11 says, *"For the grace of God that
bringeth salvation hath appeared to all men."*

Right now God's grace is appearing to all men bringing salvation. The sinner doesn't have to earn or deserve salvation. God's salvation is free. It is a gift in His hand. God is always "aggressing" toward him with salvation. And when the sinner responds, God is glorified.

The same analogy is set up in the husband and wife relationship. Look at 1 Corinthians 11:7: *"For a man indeed ought not to cover his head, forasmuch as he is the image and glory of God: but the woman* [wife] *is the glory of the man* [husband]." This does not mean that every woman is the glory of every man. It means the wife is the glory of her husband. Jesus Christ is glorified in His church, and the husband is glorified in his wife. The husband is used in the marriage relationship to typify Jesus Christ. The husband is the aggressor. The woman is the responder.

God is always aggressing, always abounding, and is glorified when we respond to Him. He *agapes* toward us, and we *phileo* back to Him. *Agape* love is glorified in our *phileo* love to Him. In the Bible, a woman is never told to *agape* her husband. Titus 2:4 says, *That they* [older women] *may teach the young women to be sober, to love their husbands, to love their children.* Both times in that verse the Greek for *"love"* is *phileo*. Wives, respond in *phileo* love to your husbands.

In contrast, every time the husband is told to love his wife, the Greek word *agape* is used. Do you know what that means? Husbands, you are to love your wife as Jesus loves the church. You are to love her whether she looks pretty or not, whether she deserves it or not.

In the Bible, young Christians are never commanded to love God. When you first become born again, you have no capacity to *agape* the Lord, you can only *phileo* Him. There are Christians today, just born again, singing, "Oh, How I Love Jesus." Do you know why they love Him? Because He answers their prayers, gives them possessions, and supplies all their needs. That is *phileo* love, a responsive love. Their love is based on something done to them.

You can tell when you have moved from *phileo* love to *agape* love with the Lord when you no longer love Him because He does things for you but simply because He is your Father. He is God. You would love Him even if He never gave you anything else. That is mature love, *agape* love. This type of love comes through more knowledge of Him.

It is the same way with husband and wife. When they first get married, they think they could never be more in love than they are at that moment. But several years down the road, they begin to realize that what they had in the beginning was just puppy love compared to what they have now. The more a husband gets to know his wife, the more he loves her. The more a wife gets to know her husband, the more she loves him.

The more I get to know my heavenly Father, the more my *phileo* love matures into *agape*. I can only experience this type of intimacy with Him through His Word. I have the ability in me to love God. His nature has been infused into my nature, and His nature can flow out from me. I now have the inner ability to love people the same way God loves me. I can now love people despite what they do or don't do. If they love me or slap me, it doesn't change me because I have *agape* love for them. *Agape* love is based on my nature, not theirs.

The world can't have *agape* love because it is a supernatural love. The best the world can have is *phileo*, a rapport love. God likes *phileo* love. He likes you to be friends with Him. He enjoys being a friend with you. The world says, "I'll love you if you will love me. Treat me right, and I will treat you right." But what happens when one fails the other? The whole basis for the relationship crumbles. Too many marriages are built on *phileo* love. God has promised believers a supernatural marriage in Ephesians 5, a marriage that will not fall apart even in the worst of circumstances, when it is based on His example of *agape* love.

Verse 22

Wives, submit yourselves unto your own husbands, as unto the Lord.

Submission is a most misunderstood word. It has been abused and misused until many people today shy away from the use of the word. The problem comes from a lack of understanding the difference between submission and obedience. They are not the same.

Submission is an attitude. Obedience is an act. When a husband demands that his wife submit, he usually is telling her to obey. The husband has turned into a dictator, a tyrant, or a master. Jesus is never a dictator. A wife does not have to obey, but she is to submit at all times. If the husband demands that the wife not go to church, she should still go. In love, she should respectfully decline his demand.

"If ye be willing [submissive] *and obedient, ye shall eat the good of the land"* (Isaiah 1:19). Even Jesus *"humbled* [submitted] *Himself and became obedient unto death"* (Philippians 2:8). Rebellion is not a lack of obedience. Rebellion is an unsubmissive attitude in a person, even though he might obey. I would much rather a wife, employee, or congregational member be submissive and not obedient than be obedient and not submissive.

The reason we can be both submissive and obedient to the Lord is because He is always right.

We are to be submissive to our government but not necessarily always obedient (Romans 13:1–5). If our government told us not to witness anymore for Jesus, we should not obey it. That violates God's command to us in Mark 16:15. We should still be submissive towards them and not rebel. The disciples faced this same situation, as we find recorded in Acts 5:27–29 and 5:40–42.

The best marriage exists when the husband does not violate God's Word in his headship to the home. Many husbands do not give their wives anything to respect. Even submission becomes difficult. The main responsibility in the home is on the husband to love and provide for the wife as Jesus does for the church. The wife can then submit and obey in all things.

"Wives, submit yourselves unto your own husbands as unto the Lord." The husband is her lord in the natural (1 Peter 3:6), just as Jesus is her Lord in the spiritual realm. A wife is privileged: She has two lords. When a wife quits fighting her husband and submits to his lordship, she becomes doubly blessed and protected. This again puts much responsibility on the husband to treat the wife as Jesus does the

church. Husbands, give your wives something
to submit to.

An Analogy

Verse 23

*For the husband is the head of the wife,
even as Christ is the head of the church:
and he is the savior of the body.*

The Greek word for *"savior"* means
"provider of everything." Just as Jesus Christ
is the Head of the church, the husband is the
head of the wife. Both the husband and Jesus
Christ are the providers of everything for their
bride. The husband should provide love, protection, finances, comfort, companionship, and
conversation. That is what Jesus provides for
His church.

Verse 24

*Therefore as the church is subject
[submissive] unto Christ, so let the wives
be to their own husbands in every thing
[every situation].*

Again, submission is always commanded in
the Word. Husbands should never use this

verse to abuse their wives. This verse is not teaching obedience in everything; instead, it teaches submission. Wives are always to maintain a correct attitude of submission.

Verse 25

Husbands, love [agape] *your wives, even as Christ also loved* [agape] *the church, and gave himself for it* [her].

The Greek word here is not *"it"* but "her." Jesus Christ gave Himself for the church and there should be such an undying love in the husband-wife relationship that the husband gives himself for the wife in everything. When you give yourself, you give everything that belongs to you. It belongs to the whole family. Jesus never hoards anything. I am a joint (equal) heir with Jesus and an heir of God the Father (Romans 8:17). Likewise, everything that belongs to the husband belongs to the wife and family.

Verse 26

That he might sanctify and cleanse it with the washing of water by the word.

The Greek word for *"word"* is *rhema*. *Rhema* is the spoken word of God. We are cleansed by the *rhema*, the spoken word of God. When we were born again, we were cleaned by the word of God. The communicating of the word of God produces faith, for *"faith cometh by hearing, and hearing by the word* [rhema] *of God"* (Romans 10:17). When you speak the word of God, you are cleaned by it.

The husband should speak words to edify the wife and encourage her. She will receive correction quickly when she is constantly encouraged for her strengths. Love-making begins with words. Edification during the day brings satisfaction at night. Jesus Christ makes love to His church through the Word. When we receive His Word, He is glorified. There are many analogies in the Word of God between the sexual relationship of a husband and wife and God's love relationship with us through His Word.

Verse 27

That he might present it [her] *to himself a glorious church, not having spot, or wrinkle, or any such thing; but that it* [she] *should be holy and without blemish.*

Rhema takes out spots and wrinkles. Marriages break down when communication breaks down. Fellowship breaks down because communication is cut off. As long as husbands and wives talk out their problems and differences and keep love as the motivating factor, they can work out all of their spots and wrinkles. The little foxes spoil the vine. Jesus' end result for the church will be glorious. Forever we will be with Him in heaven, purified and cleansed, without spot or blemish.

The church will not be totally without spot or blemish until we have gone through the judgment seat of Christ. Then, and only then, will all of the wood, hay, and stubble be burned out, and gold, silver, and precious stones be all that remain. There will be those in the church who have followed the Lord in a deeper way than others who will be as close to perfection on earth as possible. At all times in the church there will also be a large number of new converts who will be babies, as well as carnal believers. The church as a whole will reach total perfection at the rapture when we all receive resurrection bodies, which will be without the nature of the flesh, and then stand before His throne to be judged.

Verse 28

So ought men to love their wives as their own bodies. He that loveth his wife loveth himself.

Husband, you wash your body and keep it clean. Your wife is as much a part of you as your arm or leg. She belongs to you and is a part of you. You became one flesh when you accepted each other in marriage, just as you became one spirit when you accepted the Lord Jesus Christ in salvation. You, as the church, are the body of Christ. When Jesus loves you, He loves Himself. When the husband loves the wife, he loves himself.

Verses 29-30

[29] For no man ever yet hated his own flesh; but nourisheth and cherisheth it, even as the Lord the church.
[30] For we are members of his body, of his flesh, and of his bones.

Husband, just as you take care of your own body by giving it food and love, you should take care of your wife in the same way. You are to see to it that all of her needs are supplied.

The marriage relationship also helps us to understand the Godhead. How can God be three yet one? How can a husband and wife be two individuals yet one unit? The husband and wife are two separate people, but they have been joined in marriage to think and react alike.

God is three separate and distinct individuals—Father, Son, and Holy Spirit—yet, He is one in His thinking and reactions. All of the members of the Godhead make up a team. Just as a sports team is made up of many members, still they all strive for the same goal. Each plays his part to attain that goal.

Jesus is not me, and I am not Jesus. However, we are joined together at the point of the new birth as the Head and the body. This is the same thing that happens in marriage.

Verse 31

For this cause shall a man leave his father and mother, and shall be joined unto his wife, and they shall be one flesh.

"This cause" is the joining together and becoming one flesh. Marriage is the very first teaching given in the Word of God. The Lord gave instructions to Adam and Eve that the man was to leave (the authority of) his father and mother and cleave to his wife (Genesis 2:24). I think it is interesting that in-laws were told to stay out of the couple's affairs before in-laws existed.

"And shall be joined unto his wife" is a direct reference to sex. Sexual relationship is the

physical expression of being one flesh. You and
I have communion with the Lord because we
are one spirit with Him. The daily intake of the
Word of God and praying in the Spirit is an
outward expression that we are born again. Sex
is for marriage only. Praying in the Spirit, worship, and praise are for believers only.

Verse 32

*This is a great mystery: but I speak con-
cerning Christ and the church.*

This doesn't mean that this is some mys-
terious thing that cannot be understood. To the
contrary, it means that this is a dynamic mystery. Marriage helps us to understand a tremendous spiritual revelation. God's infinite
love can be more easily understood through the
relationship of a husband and wife.

Husbands, what if Jesus treated the
church like you treat your wives? What if we
treated Jesus like wives treat their husbands?
It makes you stop and think. Jesus has set up
an analogy in the natural world to show a
spiritual truth. Women should submit to their
husbands just as they submit to Jesus Christ;
husbands should love their wives just as Jesus
loves the church. With that kind of relationship, the marriage cannot do anything but

succeed. No devil can break up that marriage because Jesus said, "*I will build my church; and the gates of hell shall not prevail against it*" (Matthew 16:18). With that kind of marriage relationship, divorce is not an option.

Verse 33

Nevertheless let every one of you in particular [as individuals] so love his wife even as himself; and the wife see that she reverence her husband.

"*Reverence*" means "honor, respect, and admire." Wives, just as you honor, respect, and admire the Lord Jesus, you are to envision and love your husband. Look at your husband and imagine that you are looking at Jesus, the provider of everything. Look at him in faith. You can have what you believe God for.

Husband, start loving your wife as Jesus loves the church. She belongs to you. She is part of you.

11

Please the Lord

Ephesians 6:1–9

In this last chapter of the Book of Ephesians, we now take the message from the heart of God to the world. Every one of us is called into full-time Christian service. We do not find the terminology "clergy" and "layman" in the Bible. Just because a person sits in the congregation doesn't mean he is any less in the full-time ministry than the minister standing in the pulpit. If you go to a job and do it as unto the Lord, you are in full-time service for the Lord. You will be rewarded accordingly in heaven just as the prophet or evangelist.

The pastor cannot be in all places at the same time. The prophet can't be in more than one place at a time. God saves businessmen to witness to businessmen, factory workers to witness to factory workers, students to witness to students, and housewives to witness to housewives. He has born-again believers in all levels of society to witness for the Lord on their level. This is what causes true revival in a nation and strengthens the country from the inside out.

Verse 1

Children, obey your parents in the Lord:
for this is right.

Wives are to submit, but children are to obey. Submission demands knowledge. Children do not know enough to submit, so they are commanded to obey their parents. Understanding will come through maturity. The obligation is on the parent to properly *"train up a child"* (Proverbs 22:6) *"in the Lord."* To train them in the Word, parents must know the Word.

Verse 2

Honor thy father and mother; which is
the first commandment with promise.

Children may not understand the decisions the parents make, but they are to honor their parents. Honoring of parents brings the two-fold blessing found in Exodus 20:12. This promise is quoted in verse 3.

Verse 3

That it may be [become] *well with thee, and thou mayest live long on the earth.*

The Greek word for *"well"* means good or prosperous. *"That it may* [become prosperous] *with thee"* applies to every area of life. (See Psalm 1:1–3 and Joshua 1:7–8.) Also, divine health is promised for obedience and honor to parents. Prosperity and divine health begin at a young age and should continue through our lifetime as we grow in God's Word. *"Beloved, I wish above all things that thou mayest prosper and be in health, even as thy soul prospereth"* (3 John 2). Wisdom is said to have a long life in her right hand and riches and honor in her left (Proverbs 3:16).

Rebellion against parents is rebellion against authority. Rebellion against authority is rebellion against the Lord. God established the principles of authority for you to respect the ones over you. You may not agree with them, but you are to respect them. Children may not agree with their parents, but they are to respect, admire, and obey them.

Verse 4

And, ye fathers [parents], *provoke not your children to wrath: but bring them up in the nurture and admonition of the Lord.*

This verse is actually talking to parents. *"Provoke not your children to wrath"* means not to aggravate them. Children become angry when they are corrected or disciplined without instruction as to why. *"But bring them up in the nurture* [discipline] *and admonition* [instruction] *of the Lord."* When children are disciplined, they should be told what they did wrong before they are disciplined, and what the Word teaches about discipline afterwards.

The Word of God teaches that children should be disciplined with a paddle. (See Proverbs 13:24; 19:18; 22:15; 23:13; 29:15, 17.) This drives the foolishness out of their hearts so they can receive the instruction of the Word of God. When I spank my children, I wait until the crying is over and instruct them from Ephesians 6:1–3. I let them know that I love them and that I am disciplining them for their own benefit. I want them to grow up to be prosperous and healthy. Parents, train your children in the discipline and instruction of the Lord.

Verse 5

Servants, be obedient to them that are your masters according to the flesh, with fear and trembling, in singleness of your heart, as unto Christ.

Today, servants and masters are employees and bosses, labor and management. *"According to the flesh"* means that bosses have no right to dictate to their employees in spiritual matters. They are only bosses in the flesh over natural matters. If the boss tells you to go sweep out the storeroom, you have to do it. But if he tells you to miss church to work, you should respectfully decline. You need to draw a line and stand up for your rights in the Lord.

I want to clear up an area here about doing your job as unto the Lord. God first of all called you to that job to work productively. He did not call you there to witness when you should be working. Witness on your own time. I know of people who were fired for witnessing on the job when they should have been working. They think they are being persecuted for the gospel's sake. No, they are being persecuted for their own stupidity. How hard they work is a witness for the Lord. Spirit-filled workers should out-produce everyone on the job. They should arrive sooner than anyone else and stay later.

The word *"fear"* means "respect." It comes from the Greek word *tromos* meaning "maximum exertion or effort." So how are you supposed to serve your boss? With respect and maximum effort. Christians should be the hardest workers and have the best attitudes.

"In singleness of your heart as unto Christ" means you should have one goal in mind, pleasing the Lord. You really are working for a greater Boss, the Lord Jesus. You are doing your job unto the Lord. If Jesus were standing beside you, would you work harder? He is and you should. If you do your job as unto the Lord, you will not only get your paycheck, you will get rewards in heaven. A paycheck is for the moment. Rewards in heaven are eternal.

Now, here's the clincher.

Verse 6

Not with eyeservice, as menpleasers; but as the servants of Christ, doing the will of God from the heart.

Do you know what *"eyeservice"* is? It is working when the boss is looking and not working when he is absent. How many times have you heard (or said), "Look busy, here comes the boss!" There is always someone around even if your boss is not there, and that is the Lord.

If you are working for the Lord, you will exert as much effort when the boss is away as when he is there. If you please the Lord, you will please your boss. If you cannot please the boss by pleasing the Lord, you shouldn't be working there in the first place.

If you need a raise or promotion, don't butter up the boss. Don't be *"menpleasers."* Go to your greater Boss, the One who is higher than men, and present your request to Him. If you have been pleasing to Him, He will see to it that you get a raise. He will get you a promotion, either on that job or a better one.

> [6] *For promotion cometh neither from the east, nor from the west, nor from the south.*
> [7] *But God is the judge: he putteth down one, and setteth up another.*
>
> (Psalm 75:6–7)

Verse 7

With good will doing service, as to the Lord, and not to men.

Eunoia, the word translated *"good will,"* means "loyal enthusiasm." This means to have your mind on your job and the dedication of

your soul. This is how to get away from being
"menpleasers" and working with *"eyeservice."*

Verse 8

Knowing that whatsoever good thing
any man doeth, the same shall he receive
of the Lord, whether he be bond or free.

Notice here, *"whether he be bond or free,"*
means whether you are the boss or the employee. Whatever good thing you do, you shall
receive a reward from the Lord. It doesn't matter what position it is, the Lord will reward you
according to what you did with what you had.
"For unto whomsoever much is given, of him
shall much be required" (Luke 12:48). *"Thou*
hast been faithful over a few things, I will make
thee ruler over many things" (Matthew 25:23).

Verse 9 speaks to bosses. Spirit-filled
bosses should be the best employers.

Verse 9

And, ye masters [bosses], do the same
[equal] things unto them [employees],
forbearing threatening; knowing that
your Master also is in heaven; neither is
there any respect of persons with him.

In other words, "Bosses, treat all of your employees equally. Don't play favorites." The word *"forbearing"* means stop. Stop threatening! Don't bully your employees! If they are not doing their jobs, correct them and encourage them. Remember you also have a boss in heaven, Jesus. He runs the body of Christ, treating each member equally. Treat your employees as Jesus treats you.

Beginning with chapter 5, verse 20, and continuing through the verse above (6:9), we have been talking about the Spirit-filled life making us better wives, husbands, teenagers, employees, and bosses. Paul has dealt with the natural side of our everyday life. Next, he discusses witnessing through the weapons of our warfare, and his final topic is prayer.

12

Weapons for War

Ephesians 6:10-17

Verse 10 of chapter 6 is transitional. It introduces us to the conclusion of the book. We now come into the life of witnessing. We are about to take up the weapons of our warfare. The reasons the weapons are saved until the end of the book is because the devil hits you the hardest when you spread the gospel. The whole book has been preparing and maturing the saints to be effective soldiers to stop the enemy and recover prisoners.

It is beautiful how this book has brought the revelation all the way from one person, God the Father, through the Son and the Holy Spirit, then through all the ministry offices, and into the body. Now the body can take the message out to the world and win others to the Lord. This is where we do our combat. We come against the devil head-on because he is blinding the minds of the sinners.

Verse 10

Finally [in conclusion], *my brethren, be strong in the Lord, and in the power of his might.*

The Greek words in this verse should be old friends by now. *"Power"* is the Greek word *kratos*, "ruling power." The word *"might"* is the Greek word *ischus*, "endowed power." Ruling power refers here to stability in life. Be stabilized, having the inner power which keeps you always upright. Ruling power is on the inside of your spirit. That ruling power was endowed to you the moment you accepted Jesus Christ as your Savior.

Verse 11

Put on the whole [complete] *armor of God, that ye may be able to stand against the wiles* [strategy] *of the devil.*

This verse is in the imperative mood. It is a command, so you have no option. Paul is, at this time, an ambassador in chains. As he was writing this letter, he was confined in a Roman jail with two guards outside. He could look at the soldiers and see their armor. Roman armor did not cover the whole body like that of the knights in the Dark Ages. There were specific pieces of armor. The Lord revealed to him, through the Spirit, the armor believers have in the spiritual realm. Paul was writing this from firsthand experience.

He tells us to *"put on the whole armor of God that* [we] *may be able to stand."* The word *"able"* here is in the continuous present tense, meaning that we might continue to stand. *"Stand"* means "to hold your ground." Against what? Against the wiles (strategy or tactics) of the devil. Paul is using military terms.

This verse parallels Galatians 5:1: *"Stand fast* [hold your ground] *therefore in the liberty wherewith Christ has made us free."* This also is a military term meaning, "Once you have taken the high ground, hold onto it. Plant your flag. Don't budge!"

Put on the armor so that once you conquer the ground, you can stay. This is the devil's world, but the church is conquering and occupying new ground each day. We are marching to a victory and from a victory. Jesus conquered Satan at the cross, and we are enforcing the victory after the cross.

Verse 12

For [because] *we wrestle* [do combat]
*not against flesh and blood, but against
principalities, against powers, against
the rulers of the darkness of this world,
against spiritual wickedness in high
places.*

We are to take the offensive. *"Flesh and
blood"* refers to human beings. We do not fight
men. We fight the demon powers which back
them. Our weapons are spiritual in order to
destroy spiritual beings. Only flesh and blood
are fought with physical weapons.

[3] *For though we walk in the flesh, we do
not war after the flesh:*
[4] *(For the weapons of our warfare are
not carnal, but mighty through God to
the pulling down of strong holds;)*
[5] *Casting down imaginations, and every
high thing that exalteth itself against the
knowledge of God, and bringing into
captivity every thought to the obedience
of Christ.*   (2 Corinthians 10:3-5)

In prayer, we are not really praying for the
kings who are in authority. We are praying
against the demon influences over them and for

the angels to surround and protect them. Our prayer is binding and loosing: binding the forces of the devil and loosing the powers of the Lord. We want them to be influenced by the Holy Spirit instead of by evil spirits.

Just as in any military organization, demons have rank. Know your enemy. The Word warns us not to be ignorant of the devil's devices. Satan has his forces organized. This verse begins with the lowest of the demons and moves up to the more powerful in control.

First of all, we have *"principalities,"* which is the Greek word *arche*. These are the demons or familiar spirits who possess unbelievers and oppress believers. The demons above this control the lower ranks. These are the *"powers,"* *exeusia*, or authorities. These are the sergeants. Next are the *"rulers of the darkness of this world."* The Greek literally reads "world rulers of this darkness." The *"world"* here is *kosmos* which means "world's system." The rulers of the darkness of this world are the demons that influence kings. The last ones mentioned are *"spiritual wickedness in high places."* The Greek says "wicked spirits in the heavenlies." These are the demons that control nations. These are just under Satan himself.

The devil is an organizer. He is organized because his example came from the Lord. As Lucifer, he was over the angels and just under

the Godhead in authority. He is a counter-
feiter. He can only pervert what he learned
from God.

Verse 13

> *Wherefore* [because of Satan's organiza-
> tion] *take unto you* [pick up] *the whole
> armor of God, that ye may be able to
> withstand in the evil day* [the day of at-
> tack], *and having done all, to stand.*

The weapons God has given to us are in
front of us. We don't have to go and find them.
We just have to pick them up! *"That ye may be
able to withstand* [hold your ground] *in the evil
day"* The evil day refers to any day in which
you are under attack and facing temptation.

"And having done all" is the Greek word
katergazomai, which means "something on the
inside working itself out." This refers to the
inward power of the Holy Spirit and precise
Scriptures which are brought to the surface
through faith. Inward power becomes outward
endurance to stand and win every battle.

It is important that you pick up the armor
and put it on. It is also important to pull out
everything that is stored in you. Once you have
done all of these things in order to be able to
stand, stand. What good would it do to have all

the armor in place, be prepared to stand, and
then not stand? How many people today have
been only hearers of the Word? They are prepared to stand, but they just won't do it.

Verse 14

*Stand therefore, having your loins girt
about with truth, and having on the
breastplate of righteousness.*

The word *"stand"* means "to oppose" or
"to resist." The devil is coming against you;
oppose and resist him. You know that if you
"resist the devil, he will flee from you" (James
4:7). *"Having your loins girt"* means having
your waist buckled. This refers to the belt that
went around the waist. This belt covered a gap
where the joints of the armor met.

The loins refers to the emotions. *"Gird up
the loins of your mind"* (1 Peter 1:13). In Ephesians 4:32, we were to be *"tenderhearted"* or
have "good bowels." *"Bowels"* is used for the
emotions in 2 Corinthians 6:12. We are not to
let our emotions rule us. We are to rule our
emotions with the Word of truth (John 17:17).
A soldier must not be emotional during battle.
He can be killed if he does not keep his head.

*"And having on the breastplate of right-
eousness."* Righteousness is an attribute of your

re-created spirit. Righteousness is part of the inner man. What does the breastplate cover? It covers your chest. That is where your spirit man is, on the inside. You are to cover the chest, the area of faith. Your *"breastplate"* is having a righteousness conscience, always being aware of your position in Christ.

Verse 15

And your feet shod [tied] *with the preparation of the gospel of peace.*

"Shod" means "tied or bound up." To tie your shoes is to have your feet shod. The gospel is "good news." The gospel of peace is the message of reconciliation (Ephesians 2:14–17). We have been given the ministry of reconciliation that Jesus Christ preached. He came to preach reconciliation on the earth, *"not imputing their trespasses against them, and hath given to us the word* [message] *of reconciliation"* (2 Corinthians 5:19). The word *"reconciliation"* means "peace."

"And your feet shod with the preparation of the gospel of peace" is another reference to walking. It means, "Go and do something." In Isaiah 52:7, we read, *"How beautiful upon the mountains are the feet of him that bringeth good tidings, that publisheth peace."* Your feet

are beautiful when they bring the message of peace or reconciliation. True peace is a monopoly, possessed only by Christians. If a person accepts Christ, he can have the peace we preach. (See Romans 10:15.)

Verse 16

Above all [most important], *taking the shield of faith, wherewith* [with which] *ye shall be able to quench all the fiery darts* [flaming missiles] *of the wicked* [one].

The shield here is a door-shaped shield that a Roman soldier carried. It was large enough to hide his entire body. Light in weight, it was carried in front of him and stood about as tall as the man himself. The man simply got behind it. That is the shield of faith that we use to stand against the devil. Faith is produced from your inner man and is big enough to cover your entire body. This shield is most important because it is movable. Each other piece is for a specific part of the body. The shield can work with each part or on its own.

Take the shield of faith, *"wherewith ye may be able to quench* [extinguish] *all the fiery darts of the wicked one."* A fiery dart is a flaming missile shot at us by Satan. We often think

of a fiery dart as something thrown like a dart
at a dart board. Nothing could be farther from
the truth. These missiles will kill you and many
more people at the same time.

Here again is an analogy from the ancient
world. The armies would have large balls
(about the size of bowling balls) and would set
them on fire. They would put them in a large
catapult. Once the catapult was released, the
flaming ball would shoot up into the air for
great distances of a half-mile or more. When
they landed in a city, they could do great dam-
age to property and lives. This would save a lot
of manpower. Armies could stay a safe distance
from a city and still do much destruction.

Faith will handle Satan's largest weapons.
Again , this is why faith is most important.

Verse 17

*And take the helmet of salvation, and
the sword of the Spirit, which is the
word of God.*

First Thessalonians 5:8 says, *"But let us,
who are of the day, be sober, putting on the
breastplate of faith and love; and for an helmet,
the hope of salvation."* The helmet covers the
head, which is the soul. The breastplate covers
the chest area. Notice that it says faith is the

breastplate, but hope is the helmet. Faith is of your spirit, and hope is of the mind.

Most people minimize the mind so much, because they do not realize that your mind needs to work in conjunction with your spirit. If your mind is closed, your spirit cannot empower you. The two need to work together. Hebrews 11:1 says, *"Now faith is the substance of things hoped for."* You hope for something in your mind, but when you put faith with it from your spirit, it gives your hope substance. Faith from your spirit will take what is in your mind and give it substance. It will bring it to pass. First of all, you hope to get saved. Faith then comes by hearing the Word of God (Romans 10:17) and is combined with the hope of salvation. The reality takes place as you become a new creature. The same works for healing, financial blessing, and all other areas of the believer's walk.

It is important never to give up hope. If you do, your faith has nothing to give substance to. That is where the devil will attack you. He will try to get you to abandon hope. I know a lot of people who know the Word of God is powerful to answer their needs, but they are tired of standing and have given up hope. They know the Word will change their circumstances, but they are tired of fighting. Their faith has nothing to give substance to. The

Word says you can become *"wearied and faint in your minds"* (Hebrews 12:3). Giving up hope is becoming discouraged, weary in well doing. You will reap in due season, if you do not faint or give up hope (Galatians 6:9).

"And the sword of the Spirit, which is the word of God." The Greek word for *"sword"* is *machaira*. To understand what a *machaira* was, we need to look again into the ancient world at the different kinds of swords warriors used then. The barbarians who came against the Romans used a sword called a *rhomphaia*. This was a large sword, very wide and very long. They were so big that the men carried them across their shoulders. Many times, the blade was so large that two men had to carry one sword. When they used it, they would swing it around and possibly cut off four or five heads at one time.

The problem with this sword was that you were thrown off balance while wielding it. You had to get yourself prepared, crouch back, and swing. You were vulnerable in two positions. You were vulnerable both when you prepared your stance and after you swung the sword. It took a while to prepare, and it took time to recover. This sword was so heavy it would carry a man around with it if he was not strong enough to handle it. Soldiers had to be taught how to use this weapon.

Another sword that was used in the ancient world was the *zephos*. This sword had only a sharp point. The edges were not sharp. It was good for stabbing only. If someone was quick enough to duck, you had to pull back and strike again. This again left you vulnerable.

A third type of sword was the *akinacase*. This was used by the pirates of the ancient world. This one had only one sharp edge. You could swing in one direction only. It was good for hacking your enemy. It could be used for battle, but usually it was only ornamental. This was most popular in the ancient world as a ceremonial sword.

Another type of sword was the *dolan*. This one was disguised inside of a cane. A lot of dignitaries and noblemen used this one. If anyone tried to attack, it could be quickly pulled out and used for protection.

The Word of God is none of these. It is called a *machaira*. This was the Roman sword. It was one of the greatest inventions of the ancient world. We might call it the ICBM missile of its day. It was different from any sword ever produced. It was only 18 inches long which was very short. But not only did it have a sharp point, both sides of the blade were sharp. The soldier was never off balance because it was so light. In fact, it is said that the barbarians used to laugh as the Romans came up to attack them

with these little short swords in their hands.
But the last laugh was on the barbarians. They
were all lying dead on the sides of the hills as
the Romans walked away. No matter which
way the adversary went, the Roman could get
him. Because it had a sharp point and two
sharp edges, he could jab, cut one way, and
then the other because of its size and weight.

The barbarians mistakenly thought that
because of the immense size of their swords
they could win any fight. Size is not important,
but weight is. When a young boy plays baseball
for the first time, he always wants to use the
biggest bat. He thinks a heavy bat will knock
the ball over the fence. He has to be instructed
by his coach to get a bat suited to his size that
will not leave him off balance.

The Word of God, *machaira,* is called *"the
sword of the Spirit."* It is not a big sword that
throws you off balance. It is not something
which has only one good point (although many
ministers think it does). The Word is not ornamental.

It is not just beautiful literature to be read
at Christmas and Easter or to be left on a cof-
fee table or mantle. The Word of God does not
have a hidden meaning. It is clear. The Word is
a balanced, precision instrument designed to
destroy the devil no matter which way he
jumps in your life.

Jesus said, *"It is written"* (Matthew 4:4, 7, 10), and that is what we are to do also. Jesus was proficient at using the sword of the Spirit. The sword of the Spirit is the Word of God. *"Rhema"* is the Greek for "word" in this verse because we are to use the spoken word at the devil as Jesus did. We do not throw the Bible at the devil when he attacks; we are to take the individual promises contained in the Word and speak them at Satan in faith. This is what causes him to flee from us.

13

The Life of Prayer

Ephesians 6:18-24

We have now come to the closing part of the book of Ephesians. Here Paul points out the importance of prayer. Not only should you go out and do battle with the devil, you also should back up all action with prayer. This is where we maintain the game plan of God.

Verse 18

Praying always with all prayer and supplication in the Spirit, and watching thereunto with all perseverance and supplication for all saints.

This verse has been grossly misinterpreted. To read it as it stands in the King James, it sounds as if all types of prayer can be prayed in the Spirit, or in tongues. But the prayer of faith demands knowledge. When you pray in the Spirit, *"your understanding is unfruitful"* (1 Corinthians 14:14). Praying in the Spirit is a type of prayer itself, like the prayer of faith, the prayer of agreement, and prayer of commitment. The Greek puts the word arrangement differently in this verse and will help to explain the meaning.

The Greek literally says, "On every occasion pray with all kinds of prayer and at all times in the Spirit." There are different kinds of prayer for different situations. There is intercessory prayer, a prayer for someone else. For yourself, there is the prayer of dedication and consecration. There is the prayer of faith and the prayer of worship and thanksgiving. There is the prayer of agreement between two people for the meeting of a need (Matthew 18:19). For each occasion, there is an appropriate prayer, but any occasion is a good time for praying in the Spirit. Praying in the Spirit, or praying in tongues, edifies you and builds up your spirit to make you sensitive to know the needs of others so you can effectively pray in faith for them. (See 1 Corinthians 14:4 and Jude 20.)

Finally, all prayer should be accompanied with thanksgiving and praise (Philippians 1:4–5). When we go to God's Word and pray according to His will, we should thank Him from that moment that it is ours. Praise is faith in action.

Verse 19

And for me, that utterance may be given unto me, that I may open my mouth boldly, to make known the mystery of the gospel.

Paul wants the saints to pray for him too. Ministers, it is not wrong for you to ask your people to pray for you in areas concerning your ministry. Paul wanted these saints to pray for him for specific things. He wants to be able to speak the right words at the right time and to have boldness or confidence to speak the mystery of the gospel. Paul knew that he would meet all kinds of people who would be rough on him and oppose him. Only the Holy Spirit can give the boldness of God. Paul wanted to go and minister in the anointing of the Spirit. He asked the saints to pray for him to have that boldness.

The disciples prayed that prayer also for themselves in Acts 4:29–30: *"Grant unto thy servants, that with all boldness they may speak*

*thy word, by stretching forth thine hand to heal;
and that signs and wonders may be done by the
name of thy holy child Jesus."*

Verse 20

For which [the gospel] *I am an ambassador in bonds: that therein I may speak
boldly, as I ought to speak.*

Because Paul was bold to speak the gospel,
he was now in prison. But he asked for more
boldness! The gospel meant more to Paul than
men's threatening and confinement. He said
that, even though he was in chains, he was *"an
ambassador."* You can't chain down an ambassador for God. You can't stop him from praying. You can't stop him from writing letters
while in prison. People are bound, but God's
Word is not.

He says, *"That I may speak boldly, as I
ought to speak." "Ought to speak"* means that
he will speak at the right time. There is an important clue. You need to pray to the Lord that
you will know what to say and also know the
right time to say it. Many people think you are
to open your mouth anytime you feel like it,
and if someone gets offended, that's just too
bad. Paul here pointed out the importance of
knowing when to say the right thing.

Verses 21–22

²¹ *But that ye also may know my affairs, and how I do, Tychicus, a beloved brother and faithful minister in the Lord, shall make known to you all things:*
²² *Whom I have sent unto you for the same purpose, that ye may know our affairs, and that he might comfort your hearts.*

Tychicus was the one who delivered this letter to the Ephesians saints. As Paul is closing the letter, he says, "I am going to put this into the hands of Tychicus who is with me, and he can bring it to you. He will let you know how I am doing; when you find out, I know your hearts will be encouraged."

Verses 23–24

²³ *Peace to the brethren, and love with faith, from God the Father and the Lord Jesus Christ.*
²⁴ *Grace be with all them that love our Lord Jesus Christ in sincerity. Amen.*

Paul is ending this book in the attitude of love. He is not bitter in prison, but he still cares for the saints. He ministers peace, love with faith, and grace to them all. So be it.